A Survival Guide from a Family of Nine

Raising a G-Rated Family in an X-Rated World

Brent and Phelecia Hatch

with
Contributions by Sal Severe, Ph.D.

and
Foreword by Danny Ainge

GREENTREE PUBLISHING
Tempe, Arizona

Library of Publishers Cataloging-in-Publication Data
provided by Cassidy Cataloguing Services.

Hatch, Brent.

Raising a G-Rated Family in an X-Rated World: A Survival Guide from a Family of Nine / Brent and Phelecia Hatch; with contributions by Sal Severe; foreword by Danny Ainge.
— [2nd ed.]. — Tempe, Ariz.: Greentree Publishing, 2006.
p. cm.
Includes bibliographical references and index.
ISBN: 0-9653012-1-4
ISBN-13: 978-0-9653012-1-3
1. Child rearing. 2. Parent and child.
I. Hatch, Phelecia. II. Title.
HQ760 .H88 2006
649/.1—dc22 0507

Greentree Publishing
P.O. Box 27672
Tempe, AZ 85285
www.howtobehave.com

Project management by Cecily Markland, Gilbert, Arizona
Editing by Via Press, LLC, Encinitas, California
Design by Sample Design, Del Mar, California
Proofreading by Dawn Mayeda, Encinitas, California
Indexing by Nan Badgett, Tucson, Arizona

Printed in the United States of America
1 2 3 4 5 6 7 8 9 10

As a father of 6 children, and a grandfather of 22, I can tell you this is one great practical book of helpful hints, guides and honest suggestions.

—Senator Orrin Hatch

Raising a G-Rated Family in an X-Rated World gives us a value-filled beacon of hope to a world where the mass media inundates children's minds with its own brazen agenda. At the cynosure of parenting, Brent and Phelecia Hatch bring us back to traditional values, encouraging parents to raise children with healthy communication, nurturing discipline and, above all, love and attention.

—Kenneth W. Starr
Dean and Professor of Law, Pepperdine University

This book is full of [illegible]ionable advice with which you can enable your children to not only survive, but radiate goodness rooted in true character. Read it, stand up, take charge and move your family in the right direction!

—Tom McDevitt, *Washington Times*

As a mother of four, I strongly agree with the Hatches that communicating with our children is essential. The Band-Aid Magnet is brilliant.

—Marlee Matlin, Academy Award winning actress

Juggling life as a pro baseball player and a father of eight children can be challenging beyond words, every single day. In my profession, I had coaches that helped me see what I needed to do, how to do it, and how I could be better. As a parent, it is not always easy to find a coach for parenting your family when you need it. For that, my wife and I look for resources like this book. This book gives you the Hatches as your parenting coaches.

—Dale Murphy, Pro baseball player, Atlanta Braves, (retired)

Not only do I recommend this book if you are a parent, hope to be, or are raising children for any reason, I suggest you purchase a supply of the books and have them ready to give to your friends...This book is filled with positive results, and more importantly, with great love.

—Dottie Walters, CSP, International Speaker, Author, *Speak & Grow Rich*,
President, Walters International Speakers Bureau

This book is a must for raising kids.

—John F. Cosgrove, *Unsolved Mysteries*

For parents, this book is a necessity and an inspiration. Must reading for all parents who want their child to reach their potential, despite the media's fight to distract them.

—Vincent M. Fortanasce, M.D.,
Author, *Life Lessons from Little League: A Guide for Parents and Coaches*

Growing up, my parents instilled in me many of the same principles that Brent and Phelecia Hatch outline in *Raising a G-Rated Family in an X-Rated World.*

As an adult I can truly appreciate the work and sacrifices that my parents made to shield me from the social standards that surround us daily. I urge each and every parent to make an investment in their children and read this book. Your children will thank you, just as I thank my parents, for the lasting impression that you will make on them.

—Jessie Conners, *The Apprentice*, Season 1

Well worth the short time it takes to read this book. As a parent, it is worth a second and third read. Practical, basic, and filled with refreshing, uncommon common sense. Nothing is as important as raising the future generation to be better than the existing generation: An incredible challenge this book can help meet.

—Daryl Gates, Chief, Los Angeles Police Department (retired)

Simple rules, charming insights. The ABC's of parenthood from practicing parents.

—Richard M. Hollcraft, M.D.

The common sense that is so uncommon at this time.

—Karen Willis, Registered nurse

A timely and compelling proposal on the positive effects of nurturing within a family structure. Brent and Phelecia Hatch have a thoughtful, commonsense approach to how we can better parent our children to become successful adults.

—Vianne Castellano, Ph.D., Child/adolescent clinical psychologist

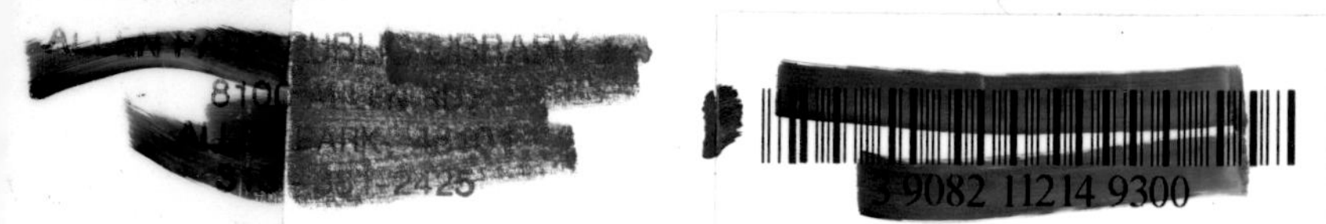

As a father of 6 children, and a grandfather of 22, I can tell you this is one great practical book of helpful hints, guides and honest suggestions.

—Senator Orrin Hatch

Raising a G-Rated Family in an X-Rated World gives us a value-filled beacon of hope to a world where the mass media inundates children's minds with its own brazen agenda. At the cynosure of parenting, Brent and Phelecia Hatch bring us back to traditional values, encouraging parents to raise children with healthy communication, nurturing discipline and, above all, love and attention.

—Kenneth W. Starr
Dean and Professor of Law, Pepperdine University

This book is full of wisdom, encouragement and actionable advice with which you can enable your children to not ony survive, but radiate goodness rooted in true character. Read it, stand up, take charge and move your family in the right direction!

—Tom McDevitt, *Washington Times*

As a mother of four, I strongly agree with the Hatches that communicating with our children is essential. The Band-Aid Magnet is brilliant.

—Marlee Matlin, Academy Award winning actress

Juggling life as a pro baseball player and a father of eight children can be challenging beyond words, every single day. In my profession, I had coaches that helped me see what I needed to do, how to do it, and how I could be better. As a parent, it is not always easy to find a coach for parenting your family when you need it. For that, my wife and I look for resources like this book. This book gives you the Hatches as your parenting coaches.

—Dale Murphy, Pro baseball player, Atlanta Braves, (retired)

Not only do I recommend this book if you are a parent, hope to be, or are raising children for any reason, I suggest you purchase a supply of the books and have them ready to give to your friends…This book is filled with positive results, and more importantly, with great love.

—Dottie Walters, CSP, International Speaker, Author, *Speak & Grow Rich*,
President, Walters International Speakers Bureau

This book is a must for raising kids.

—John F. Cosgrove, *Unsolved Mysteries*

For parents, this book is a necessity and an inspiration. Must reading for all parents who want their child to reach their potential, despite the media's fight to distract them.

—Vincent M. Fortanasce, M.D.,
Author, *Life Lessons from Little League: A Guide for Parents and Coaches*

Growing up, my parents instilled in me many of the same principles that Brent and Phelecia Hatch outline in *Raising a G-Rated Family in an X-Rated World*.

As an adult I can truly appreciate the work and sacrifices that my parents made to shield me from the social standards that surround us daily. I urge each and every parent to make an investment in their children and read this book. Your children will thank you, just as I thank my parents, for the lasting impression that you will make on them.

—Jessie Conners, *The Apprentice*, Season 1

Well worth the short time it takes to read this book. As a parent, it is worth a second and third read. Practical, basic, and filled with refreshing, uncommon common sense. Nothing is as important as raising the future generation to be better than the existing generation: An incredible challenge this book can help meet.

—Daryl Gates, Chief, Los Angeles Police Department (retired)

Simple rules, charming insights. The ABC's of parenthood from practicing parents.

—Richard M. Hollcraft, M.D.

The common sense that is so uncommon at this time.

—Karen Willis, Registered nurse

A timely and compelling proposal on the positive effects of nurturing within a family structure. Brent and Phelecia Hatch have a thoughtful, commonsense approach to how we can better parent our children to become successful adults.

—Vianne Castellano, Ph.D., Child/adolescent clinical psychologist

Dedication

To our seven wonderful children: Shane, Chari, Ashlyne, Mckay, Dakota, Saige, and Hunter. We feel so privileged to be your parents. We were able to write this book because of your love and patience and support.

To every parent who ever feels alone in raising children, remember we are all in this together. It takes a village to raise our next generation of kids.

Acknowledgement

This book was written through years of learning and doing. Many people have taught us many things along the way and have touched our lives. To all of you, we are forever grateful.

Thanks to our publisher, Tim McCormick, for sharing our vision. Thanks, too, to Karla Olson, and to Dana and Debbie Suorsa. And, to Cecily Markland, thanks for your contributions and suggestions. Thanks especially to Carin Dewhirst Knutson for never giving up. Most of all, thanks to our families. Your love and patience helped us grow.

About the Authors

Brent and Phelecia Hatch, parents, authors, and motivational speakers, are the co-creators of The Hug Card, more than 3 1/2 million sold worldwide. They also invented the "Alcohol Breath Detector Card," the Family Report Card, and the Band-Aid Magnet. The Hatches and their innovative approaches to parenting have been featured on NBC's "Today in L.A.," as well as *Parent's Guide* Magazine, and the *Pasadena Star News* and its affiliates.

In 2001 Brent and Phelecia were selected as California's Parents of the Year, and they were honored in Washington, D.C., by proclamation from President George W. Bush on National Parents Day.

The Hatches live in South Pasadena, California.

Foreword
by Danny Ainge

I believe today's real heroes aren't found on the baseball fields and basketball courts. Nor are they found in government buildings or the boardrooms of big businesses. Instead, the real heroes are good parents who work within the walls of their own homes to make a difference in the lives of their children.

In my more than 20 years in college and professional sports, I learned over and over that it's impossible to control everything that happens during a game. Instead, as a coach and a player, you have to be prepared to make adjustments; you have to plan how you will react and be ready for any situation that may arise. Those players and coaches who don't allow the game to run them, but who turn situations around to make them fit their game plan and their rules, are the ones who are truly great and who emerge as winners.

The lives of our children are much more important than any game; yet, the same thing applies in our role as parents. Faced with the onslaught of filth and degradation in the world today, parents need to take control and turn the situation around so the media and the forces in the world are not controlling what happens in our homes.

By using the ideas outlined in this book, you can be better prepared as a parent to face whatever situation may arise. The Hatches are right on and do an excellent job of explaining how you can lay down your own "ground rules," take more control, and find ways to raise children who are winners.

As you take a stand for your family and for decency, you will be doing something that is sorely needed in the world today. Best of all, you will become a real hero in the eyes of your own children.

Danny Ainge played college basketball, four years of professional baseball, and spent 14 years with the National Basketball Association, first as a player, then as a coach for the Phoenix Suns. Currently, he and his wife, Michelle, live in Boston where Danny is executive director of basketball operations for the Boston Celtics. Danny also serves on the Board of Directors of United Families International. Three of the Ainge's six children are married and three are still living at home.

Table of Contents

Introduction

Why We Bought Baby-Gates

Remember when your first child began to crawl and pull up on furniture? You watched in delight as your infant reached for low tables and chairs and proudly stood up on chubby, sturdy legs. Then the horror began.

You imagined your child crawling and pulling up on everything and realized that the wobbly, vintage table in the entry was not fastened to the wall and it supported a heavy lamp that threatened to crash down on your inquisitive toddler. Why had you never noticed the gaps between the cantilevered stairs leading to the second floor? Couldn't a tiny body squeeze between those steps and fall? You glanced outside at the new, five-foot-deep fishpond and you suddenly saw it not as a pretty decoration but a drowning hazard.

If you're like us, you baby-proofed your living space. You spent several weekends removing hazards and then bought baby-gates to create kid-safe areas. Why didn't you ignore the hazards and say to yourself: "My kids are just going to have to learn where they can go and where they can't, what they can touch and what they can't"? You didn't ignore hazards because you understood that your baby hadn't developed the physical and cognitive skills to navigate them, and it was not worth the risk of your child getting hurt. It was your job as a parent to make the living space appropriate to the baby's developmental stage.

Beyond Baby-Gates: Make Your Home a Kid-Safe Media Zone

Now your kids are older. They walk instead of crawl, and they know the difference between grandmother's vase and a plastic pitcher. They know what they can touch and what they can't, so you've unpacked your breakables and are enjoying them once again.

Yet there are other kinds of hazards lurking, dangers that your kids may not be prepared for or know how to avoid. They turn on the TV and they might witness an inappropriate behavior. They flick on the radio and suddenly bad language fills the house. The fact is, we are raising our kids during the era of the media blitz, which makes it imperative that you "media-proof" your home. Instead of removing breakables, you need to control outside influences that you feel don't represent your family's values and beliefs.

How do you do this? The first step is to become conscious of all the subtle hazards that exist. To do that, you must remove the rose-colored glasses that make your home look wholesome and G-Rated to you. Put on X-Rated-vision glasses that will reveal the potential hazards, the sources of obscenities and violence, and the places where perilous and inappropriate images, words or messages can be found in your home. These are the hazards we ignore daily because they have become so much a part of our lives that we don't think to question them.

The answer is to create a kid-safe media zone in your home. Over a period of time, do the following exercises—you need not do them all at once. Before beginning each exercise, pretend you are a visitor in your own home; try to look at your surroundings with a fresh eye. After completing each exercise, review the questions listed under the "think about it" section.

Exercises

- Walk through each room/space in your home and take note of all the printed media you leave lying around (magazines, books, newsletters, newspapers, advertising circulars, etc.). Then think about the words and pictures you observed and consider the messages your children and teens are getting from the printed media in your home.
- Watch TV with your kids. Don't influence their program choices, just sit with your kids, watch the program, and observe your kids' reactions to it.
- Watch your child or teen as they surf the Internet or play computer or video games. Again, don't interfere with where they go, what they choose, or how they react.
- Listen to the music your children or teens like. Listen to the words or read the lyrics if you can. Pay attention to how the music makes you feel—sad, happy, energetic, down, agitated, uplifted.
- Read through the magazines your children read or browse the offerings for kids and teens at the magazine stand. Try to imagine how your children would feel comparing themselves to what they see. What is presented as "cool"? What is not?

Think About It

- Do your children and teens receive mostly inappropriate or appropriate messages from the media in your home?
- Did you agree with the values presented or did they make you wince?
    - Was the level of sexual content acceptable or unacceptable to you?
    - Were the roles of men and women stereotypical?
    - Did you notice incidences of sexism or racism?

- How did people in relationships treat each other? Would you want your child to treat friends or family in this way?
    - Did the people speak to each other appropriately? Did they use language that you would allow in your home?
- Was the world depicted as generally positive or negative, as predominately peaceful or violent?
- Were your kids encouraged to "buy, buy, buy"?
- How many commercials did you watch during the show?
- Were characters judged by who they are or what they have?

What you find may surprise you, and it is important to take action if you see the need. The first thing you must understand is that you, the parent, are in control of the messages in your home. This book overflows with ideas for how to make sure that the values and ideas presented are ones you feel your children are ready to handle.

Chapter 1

"A Huge Chaotic Mess!": A Visit to the Hatch Household

We thought that writing about our life would be effortless, because writing about what you know is supposed to be easy. But when this manuscript was about six months late to our publisher, Phelecia and I had to admit that we were overwhelmed. Raising our seven kids, running a family business, and writing a parenting book—it was just too much.

That is when our editor asked, "If a filmmaker was to make a movie about your family, what would viewers see? What goes on around your house most days?" The question was designed to help us to write from a new perspective, and it was hard not to wonder what a fresh set of eyes would see, what we could no longer see, when looking at our children, our family, and our house.

Brent: *Picture 40 kids, ages five to 17, hanging out in a tiny, messy backyard. A few are in the garage playing a video game; six are shooting hoops, four are in the hot tub. There is a yell, then a shrill whistle sounds and most gather around the two kids who are fighting. The boxing gloves are heavy and awkward, and the kids really don't know all the correct moves yet, but as I coach them from the rigged-up sidelines, they start to throw punches and then get the hang of it. My own son is slight but quick and starts hammering on his opponent. I break things up and teach everyone how to call "quits" by lowering his or her head.*

Phelecia: *What does this look like to others? I bet nothing but a huge, chaotic mess!*

Yes, sometimes.

To us and to other parents we talk with, the world in which our children live is like boxing: it can be dangerous, hurtful, and chaotic. From a concerned parent's perspective, we see a society where indecency is often the norm and much of life is unsupervised. Sex and violence are often glorified, and there is diminishing respect for the core values of a caring society: civility, kindness, respect, self-discipline, community, and more. What was once scandalous and shocking is now accepted, embraced, and encouraged, and many people's central motivation is immediate self gratification.

There is no doubt that the explosion of media—TV, movies, videos, web sites, music, music videos, etc.—in our world today has contributed to this breakdown. However, we also understand that our children are fortunate to live at a time when information, culture, and global awareness are at their fingertips via media and the Internet. The opportunities of the world are open to our children as never before. There is tremendous and undeniable power and value in that.

The key is achieving balance. Face it, it is hard for adults, much less children, to balance the media's power to corrupt with its power to inform and enlighten. So the first thing we want readers to understand is that we don't feel that raising a G-Rated family means completely eliminating the media and the Internet and sheltering your kids from anything you find unacceptable in life. Keep in mind that they won't always be with you, and one day they will have to deal with these issues on their own. We choose to embrace the media, but on our terms, with awareness and supervision, so that we control what comes into our home and what influences our children.

Raising a G-Rated Family in an X-Rated World explains how we strike that balance, how we help our children develop good judgment and teach them decision-making skills, so that they can choose between right and wrong. Within reason, we will let our children box and do other "dangerous" activities. The difference is that we watch our kids and we pay attention to what they are doing. We provide guidance, we teach them to "fight fair," we steer them toward good clean fun, and we provide them with the tools and confidence they need to make their own choices. Our job is not to completely eliminate the rough spots our children might encounter; life is full of rough spots. Our job is to help them navigate through and learn how to deal with those rough spots.

In this book we begin where we always begin—with stories. As we share our stories with friends at home, with parents in seminars, and with folks in church, we hear stories about other families. We've heard about a 14-year-old girl who was disowned for wanting to stay in school. We've listened to the pain of a young boy who was addicted to pornography. We've hugged a girl who could not tell her parents she needed them to hug her. We've been reminded of our own pain when we hear about children who are sexually molested. We've felt the depression of being around someone who is constantly negative and critical. We've seen the harm that occurs when families cannot set limits or boundaries. As if parenting was not hard enough, we witness each day what effects the media has on children and families.

The tools and tactics presented in this book are powerful and proven—we use them to raise our own seven children, and we teach them to other parents and families. We firmly believe in the power of love, hope, and positive thinking. We also believe that by applying the strategies in this book—by taking control of your home, organizing your family life, improving the way you talk to your kids, and incorporating positive discipline techniques in your routine—you can establish a loving, positive, G-Rated family of your own.

Chapter 2

"Buy, Buy, Buy - More, More, More": What the Media Tells and Sells to Your Kids

Phelecia: *It's 11:17, almost midnight. Most of our seven kids are asleep. Our oldest is up reading, but for the time being, the other six are in bed. The baby has a bad cold, so he'll be up coughing and uncomfortable in an hour or two. Since it's a balmy summer night, three of the seven children and my husband, Brent, are sleeping in a tent in the backyard. I should be asleep and not writing or I'll never keep up with them tomorrow. However, Brent and I have had to write this book late at night or very early in the morning. We learned the hard way not to write while the kids "play."*

Our editor learned the hard way as well. She told us about one Saturday when she was determined to finish editing a chapter, but her husband happened to be away at a Boy Scout-leader training. To get some time to work, she set up various activities in the house and yard for her children and for all the neighborhood kids who gather daily at her house to play. It was the usual stuff: craft supplies, a wading pool, water balloons, play dough, bubble-blowing liquid, snacks, etc. As a special treat, she let the kids have the video camera to make a movie or just have fun filming.

"It's not that I didn't supervise the kids, but I was distracted," she admitted while relating the story.

Apparently, by the end of the day, her son was directing and filming three screaming boys wearing loincloths and green body makeup. A patio chair was glued to an outdoor table with fast-drying epoxy, and the wading pool was full of birdseed. Six shoes caked on the inside with baking soda and vinegar were scattered in grainy puddles on the damp patio. In the bathroom, her four-year-old daughter and a playmate had thoroughly smeared lotion on the mirrors and stuck what appeared to be 250 bandages to the floor and walls. In the kitchen, the older kids had prepared "fun food." After dyeing carrots a deep teal-blue, they then sautéed them in maple syrup, butter, cinnamon, pebbles, and hot sauce. They froze half the batch in an ice cube tray, sprinkled the rest with crushed nuts, then accidently spilled the balance onto the Swedish, 1940's-vintage kitchen table and left it to seep onto the floor in a colorful pool.

"As I stepped in a pile of mallet-smashed walnuts, the neighbor girl walked in holding our kitten who was dripping wet after receiving a spiky 'fur-do.' Right then I realized that I should have just put on some videos," she remarked to us with a smile.

Use Media Wisely

In nine out of ten cases, we believe in limiting TV and video watching. In this case, however, we think a wholesome video and a trustworthy babysitter would, at the very least, have made clean-up easier.

We include this story for three reasons: first, it's a slice of life to which we all can relate—whether you have one child or seven children. Life gets too busy to be the perfect parent all the time, so once in while we all plunk our kids down in front of the TV or just leave them unsupervised and hope for the best. Second, this story reminds us that, as parents, we need a sense of humor. Third, parenting skills can make raising kids easier—and certainly prevent disasters such as this one!

It's your kids' job to keep you busy. It's your job to laugh at their antics when you can. And it's our job to give you some of the parenting wisdom we've learned from our seven children and two decades of parenting.

We are all raising our kids during the era we call the "media blitz." This bombardment of information and entertainment is fueled by incredible technology that allows access to the Internet from almost anywhere. Yet, Brent and I believe that all parents should be wary of any and all "electronic babysitters." Parents often ask us why we care so much about monitoring and limiting our kids' exposure to media. After all, they argue, kids learn so much from educational television shows and computer programs. This is partially true, and a recent (2003) Kaiser Family Foundation study called "Zero to Six" found that 43 percent of parents interviewed were likely to say that TV "mostly helps" young children's learning.[1] Research also indicates that most parents will *say* that their children copy the good values they see on TV, like sharing and helping, but parents also report that four-to-six-year-old boys imitate violent behavior from TV.[2] So is media good or bad? There's good media and bad media, and parents must sort that out for themselves. More importantly, parents must recognize the media's potential power to influence their children both positively and negatively.

Sex Sells

In *The Beauty Myth*, Naomi Wolf reminds readers of the power and influence of the pornography business by noting that it is a $7-billion-a-year industry.[3] While pornography is removed somewhat from mainstream media, research shows that there has been a huge increase in sexual content in the regular media—and that is very troubling. The material is so enticing that children are drawn to it. We worry that as kids see examples of violence and pornography they will think to themselves, "This is such fun; this isn't bad."

Phelecia: *Sometimes, we feel as parents that we want to hide our children in a box. We want to shelter them from unwholesome* *aspects of the world. But we have learned that is not the way that you should do it, because that can actually work against you.*

What can parents do to raise G-Rated kids in an X-Rated world? We must give our children the values and skills they need to make sound choices.

About 21 million people buy *Sports Illustrated* magazine each week.[4] Once a year, however, the weekly sales double, because the *Sports Illustrated Swimsuit Issue* features slick, sexy photos of women. The swimsuit issue sells about 55 million copies each year. According to a *Sports Illustrated* press release, "...it is the most widely read single issue of any magazine in the world." The swimsuit issue also has its own pages on the magazine's web site which, in February 2003 alone, was visited by 73 million people.[5]

Media producers understand that sex and violence attract consumers. More consumers results in higher advertising sales and, therefore, increased profits for media companies. So expect media producers to provide more sex and violence in the future, even on network TV during primetime.

According to a Kaiser Family Foundation study called "Sex On TV," "...the number of programs with sexual content rose from about half (56 percent) of all shows in the 1997/1998 television season to two-thirds (68 percent) in the 1999/2000 season. *Sexual content is even more common on the primetime network programs than on television in general.* Two years ago, two out of three (67 percent) primetime network programs included sexual content. Today, three out of four (75 percent) do."[6]

This same study finds that more teen television characters are involved in sexual intercourse. "Two years ago, 3 percent of all television characters involved in intercourse were teens; that figure is now 9 percent."[7]

Very few television programs that show or imply sexual activity say anything about the risks or responsibilities of sex. And while some TV programs depict married couples or those in a long-term relationship having sex, in 16 percent of the sex scenes the couples have just met. Kaiser Family Foundation vice president Victoria Rideout notes, "Every time there is sex on TV, there is an opportunity to deliver useful information to young people. While some shows are taking advantage of that opportunity, nine out of ten are not."[8]

Children Watch and Learn about Sex and Violence

Phelecia: *One day we got a letter in the mail addressed to our then seven-year-old son. I usually don't open his mail, but I just felt that the writing and everything about this letter was kind of suspicious. So I opened it up, and it said, "Dear______, I want to marry you and have sex with you. Love, Christina."*

How *did* Christina, a seven-year-old, learn about having sex? After talking to the school principal, we learned she had seen a TV movie with her family. As parents, it is so important to use our good judgment and make sure that we truly think about what our children will absorb from movies, TV programs, or video games. It's important to think: "What is the message of this? What is this going to say to my child?"

It is no wonder that many children are exposed to sex, violence, crass language, and more when you understand that on average, children ages 2 to 18 watch three hours of TV a day. About 80 percent of the time, parents are *not* viewing TV with their children to supervise what they watch.[9] Now consider these facts:

- More than 80 percent of all movies, sitcoms, and soap operas on TV contain sexual content.
- Primetime TV contains about five violent acts per hour.
- Saturday morning programming has about 26 violent acts per hour.[10]

Clearly, as children and teens watch TV unsupervised, they see lots of violence and sex.

What Do We Mean by X-Rated? How Do We Define G-Rated?	
X-Rated: More than Movies	***G-Rated: More than Movies***
X-Rated material includes adult and child pornography, as well as indecent language or material. Indecent material has been defined by the U.S. Supreme Court as "any language or material that depicts or describes in terms patently offensive as measured by contemporary community standards for the broadcast medium, sexual or excretory activities or organs." *F.C.C. v. Pacifica Foundation (1978)*[11] Our definition of X-Rated material includes language or material that degrades women, men, or children of any race or religion, and material that promotes or depicts excessive, gratuitous violence.	G-Rated language and material depicts or describes wholesomeness and decency. This material reflects the values shared by the community including trustworthiness, respect, responsibility, fairness, caring, citizenship, generosity, kindness, politeness, and cooperation. G-Rated material *does not* degrade women, men, or children of any race or religion, and *does not* depict or promote gratuitous violence.

According to the Center for Media Education, by the time a child completes elementary school, he or she will have witnessed 100,000 acts of violence on TV, including 8,000 murders.[12]

Teaching Kids How to Watch TV

You are probably thinking, "But I *can't* supervise or control what my kids see or hear via the media 24 hours a day and seven days a week!" No parent can supervise his/her children all the time, but discussing and critiquing what we see on TV, hear on the radio, or receive in the mail can be perfect moments to teach and learn. When you are with your children and something completely unexpected and unwanted is "in your face" via the media (remember the infamous "costume malfunction" of 2004's Super Bowl halftime show?), take time to talk to your children about what you have seen, heard, or read. Explain your feelings about it and let them share theirs. Ask to hear their opinions and take the time to share your own opinions and values.

Here are a number of ideas we have for how you can help your kids cope with TV's influence on their lives:

- Experts say, "Stick to your 'guns'" and limit TV viewing. A recent study found that children watch much less TV when parents or caregivers *set firm limits on TV watching.* The extra bonus is that these children probably read more.
- Children under two years old should *not* watch TV, according to the American Academy of Pediatrics.
- Set rules about what your children may and may not watch.
- Talk to your child/children about what they see on TV. Share your opinions on what is right and wrong.
- Do not allow children to have TVs or computers in their bedrooms, because it is more difficult to supervise and/or discuss what they are doing or seeing.

Phelecia: *Years ago, Brent and I decided our kids were watching too much TV, so we banned it during the school week, Monday through Thursday, but let them watch as much as they wanted on weekends. Frankly, it was sickening to see them in front of the TV hour after hour on Saturdays and Sundays. So after a little planning, we had a TV-free week.*

We discovered the TV habit was hard to break! The kids didn't know what to do without TV, so we got out our board games, made different kinds of play dough, played baseball, and tag—we had to get creative, but we had fun. Now, our family watches TV on the weekends, but we insist that if the kids watch TV for an hour, they must spend an hour reading or doing something creative. Our kids now read and play more than before.

Video Games

Parental supervision and family discussions should not be limited to TV watching. The average child also spends about 20 minutes a day playing video games. A recent study found that almost 90 percent of the top-selling video games portray serious violence. In most games, killing is justified and rewarded. Victims of violence in these games appear unaffected by violent attacks. The study also found that sexual stereotyping is the norm in video games. Women characters are usually depicted in revealing clothing and act as props or bystanders. Male characters are competitive and aggressive. In addition to violent content and sexual stereotyping, video games have a great deal of racial stereotyping as well.[13]

Exposure to Violence Leads to Violence

What is the result of this exposure to sex and violence in the media? Thousands of research studies done since the 1960s, indicate that some children and teens who are raised on a steady diet of violent movies, TV shows, and video games are less sensitive to the pain and suffering of others. They tend to prefer using aggression to resolve conflicts; they are more fearful of the world; and they have an increased desire for violence in entertainment and real life.[14]

Did you know?
The following respected organizations believe there is a connection between exposure to violent media and actual violent acts for some children and teens:

- American Academy of Pediatrics
- American Psychological Association
- American Medical Association
- National Institute for Mental Health[15]

Studies also show that when sex and violence are combined, as in viewing violent pornography, levels of aggression by men towards women go up. "In explicit depictions of sexual violence, it is the message about violence more than the sexual nature of the materials that appears to affect the attitudes of adolescents about rape and violence toward women."[16]

Brent: *I am not surprised that research shows how harmful violent pornography can be. For years we've heard stories of teens addicted to porn in various forms—magazines, videos, and Internet sites. The sad story usually goes like this: a kid, usually a boy, finds a "girly" magazine, adult video, or porn web site at home or at a friend's house. He likes it, wants more, and soon he's addicted. One parent told us that her son started with porn and then began molesting children. We realize that these were extreme cases of children and with severe problems. But the key seems to be supervision and open dialogue and discussion. Supervise and communicate with your kids, and you can limit their chances of hurting themselves and others.*

The Center for Media Education gives additional reasons for monitoring children and TV and video games including health problems, academic concerns, and overall quality of life issues. "Children who watch a lot of TV have a greater risk of obesity, increased alcohol and drug use, and earlier involvement in sexual activity. Children who watch four or more hours of TV per day spend less time on school work, have poorer reading skills, play less well with friends, and have fewer hobbies than children who watch less TV." [17]

Research studies can only reveal how the media affects the behavior of children, teens, and adults. We believe there are incalculable ways that children are affected. The author, Sissela Bok, raises this concern in her book, *Mayhem*. "Is it alarmist or merely sensible to ask what happens to the souls of children nurtured, as in no past society, on images of rape, torture, bombings and massacre that are channeled into their homes from infancy?"[18]

Selling Kids Violence and More

Brent: *Most of the music out there today—that is, the so-called popular, "hot" music—is not what we like to have in our house. We feel the lyrics of popular music are harmful to children. The songs often degrade women and promote violence and sex. So any of that type of music is not allowed in our house.*

Remember when "break dancing" was popular? About that time there was a song, and if you listened to it carefully it said, "Enjoy cigarettes." Music industry executives know what they are doing. They know exactly what they are trying to influence kids to do, and so there is a lot of inappropriate music out there. But we can't just say to our kids, "You are not listening to anything," because they will find it, and they will get it and listen to it if they want to. So, you have got to find a balance.

The music ratings and warnings are helpful. Stores are not supposed to sell music with mature lyrics to kids under a certain age; but a lot of them do. It is your responsibility, so if your kids like a certain band, find out more about it.

Brent: *I watched a popular rock group interviewed on television. Their whole goal was to teach kids about sex, tell them that drugs are okay, prostitution is okay. Beating your wife, killing your mother—they implied that all these things are okay. The band members said they didn't care what they were teaching young people. "We're not trying to be role models." They came out and said, "This is what we are trying to teach kids, so what? They are buying our music. Who cares?"*

As we struggle to protect our children by helping them avoid inappropriate material, the movie, music, and electronic games industries are working harder to market violent and inappropriate material to children. The Federal Trade

Commission (FTC) issued a report in September 2000 saying, "Target marketing to children of entertainment products with violent content is pervasive and aggressive." The FTC called media companies "brazen" and found that some companies had plans to promote age-restricted products at boys' and girls' clubs, a youth basketball game, and other places created to be wholesome gathering spots for young people.[19]

Advertising and marketing to children is a profitable, well-established industry.[20] For every five hours of programs that children watch on commercial TV, they see at least one hour of commercials.[21] Internet sites designed for children are full of pop-up ads, surveys, and games, all designed to sell things to children. The goal of cyberspace advertisers is to develop "brand loyalty" with children as early as possible.[22]

The problem with advertising to children is that young kids tend to believe whatever the advertisers tell them—and the more TV children watch, the more they believe in the advertising. Advertisers know that children are easily influenced, so during Saturday morning TV programs, advertisers tell children to eat sugary cereals, candy, fast food, and other junk food. Kids are also told that they must have the latest plastic toy—usually a tie-in to a TV show or movie. But advertisements for candy and toys seem less harmful compared to the almost 100,000 alcohol commercials that teens will see before they reach drinking age.[23]

As a result of all the advertising to children in the regular and digital media, the Center for Media Education has urged public debate on the subject of what constitutes media "safe zones" for children. Currently, a web site or TV show that is free of sexual or violent content is considered safe or even quality media material. But if a program or web site is simply a promotion tool for a product, is that really quality material?[24]

Help for a Never-Ending Battle

Children don't have the judgment or impulse control to cope with the examples of sex and violence readily available on the Internet, TV, video games, music videos, and music lyrics. Yet, children are exposed to harmful media and taught unwholesome lessons. Violent video games do not teach children how to resolve conflicts by listening and communicating effectively. Pornography is exploitive and does not help kids understand that sound relationships are built on emotional intimacy, caring, and kindness.

The huge amounts of sex and violence in the media make us feel that the world is X-Rated. And that is why supervising kids and communicating with them is important. Will supervising your kids and talking to them mean less time for you and the things you want to do? Yes. But good parenting skills will make your job easier and help you to enjoy your children at all stages of their development.

The strategies we will discuss in the next chapter will help you take control of your home and make it a kid-safe media zone. These are the "nuts and bolts" of raising a G-Rated family.

Chapter 3

"Welcome to My Home": Strategies for Creating a G-Rated Environment

Brent: *At some point, all children are asked to choose between right and wrong. Often, they have to make split-second decisions. We know our kids will be offered drugs. We know our children will be confronted with sexual material—perhaps on TV or via the Internet. We know our kids will make decisions about physical intimacy when they date. They won't ask us before they make many of these decisions.*

It is scary to think about the world we will send our kids into. From a parent's point of view, the real world can seem like a place full of adult material, dangerous situations, and tough choices.

We worry about the choices our children will make. "Will my son take a 'hit' from a marijuana cigarette?" "Will our daughter 'go too far' with her boyfriend?" "Will our middle child give in to peer pressure?" Let's stop right here. Take a deep breath and quit worrying so much. Worrying won't help our kids make good choices. What we need are strategies that will give kids the tools they need to make G-Rated choices.

Start by taking control of your home. While this seems like a huge job, this chapter describes four strategies that will go a long way towards taking control of your home life.

Strategy #1: Your Home as a Kid-Safe Media Zone
The key to a kid-safe zone is supervision.

Strategy #2: Family Night
This section explains Family Night and provides you with a plan for bringing your family together to sing, learn, and meditate.

Strategy #3: The Family Report Card
To help children share their true feelings and help you meet their needs, we introduce the Family Report Card.

Strategy #4: The Band-Aid Magnet
Finally, we explain The Band-Aid Magnet: an ordinary magnet for the refrigerator that is an extraordinary tool for helping children express hurt feelings.

Strategy #1: Your Home as a Kid-Safe Media Zone

We have talked to many families about how they set limits on TV and video watching, video and computer game playing, and Internet surfing. We learned that there is not just one way to set these kinds of limits. Instead, we found that parents have different styles for dealing with the media and their kids. But all these ways of limiting media had one thing in common: supervision. *In households where the kids had a healthy, reasonable exposure to various media, their parents knew what they were watching or playing and also talked about it with them.*

Limiting TV

More and more parents who attend our seminars are completely eliminating broadcast television from their households. They don't subscribe to cable or satellite TV. Parents report the following advantages to this policy:

- The entire household watches less TV.

- Children and adults read more.
- Children stop begging for the latest toy, sugary cereal, or candy because they are no longer bombarded by advertisements.
- Children are less likely to use the latest slang expressions if they don't hear them used by characters in TV shows and movies.
- Parents who do allow their children to watch videos or DVDs can easily control what their children watch.

The major drawback to cutting out TV altogether is that it can become more powerful to certain kids because it has been forbidden. Parents who have tried this found that they overcame this problem by allowing their children to watch TV when visiting friends and relatives.

We prefer to set firm limits on TV viewing rather than banning it. We believe that children can be taught to watch TV in moderation just as they can learn to eat sweets and junk food moderately.

There are also fine families that let their children watch anything on TV—as long as a parent is on hand to watch with them. We have found that these parents tend to discuss the content of the shows they watch with their children. They also teach their children not to be swayed by advertising.

One family we know loves to watch reality shows depicting ordinary people who are stranded together and also locked in a battle to outlast others and win lots of money. This family has four kids from ages 5 to 13 and the whole family watches reality shows together. Sometimes they invite the neighbors over for an outdoor reality-show-watching "block party" complete with tiki torches, food, and the TV set up on the patio. As the kids and adults watch together, they have the opportunity to talk about what they hear and see on "reality TV." The children learn what wise adults think about the activities or values portrayed on these kinds of shows.

Here are a few ideas for ways to limit TV viewing or video game playing whether you are there to supervise or not:

- Allow your children a fixed amount of "media viewing" time each day. Discuss an acceptable amount with them.
- Purchase a timer and set it when the TV, computer, or video game is turned on.
- Ask your children what they watched or played while you were not around.
- Reward them for accepting and adhering to your limits.

Controlling the Internet

What about the Internet? To protect your children from unwholesome Internet material, you need to have filters in place on your children's computer account. Most major online service providers supply tools to enable you to filter what your child sees on the web. There are also software packages that you can install on your computer to do the same thing. Follow the instructions provided by the online service provider or manufacturer. To test the filtering system, simply search on trigger words such as sex, pornography, drugs, etc.

There is no right or wrong way to make your home a kid-safe media zone, but here are a few tips we have learned from wonderful media-savvy families:

- Set limits on TV watching based on your kids' temperaments. If they are too intense or willful to accept limits without constant, annoying battles, then consider banning TV altogether. If your kids happily accept limits, you know what to do!
- Block unwholesome Internet material with filters.
- Teach your kids to ignore advertising. Tell them that when the ads come on TV, that's when they should get a snack, stretch their legs, finish a chore (right!), etc.
- Take an interest in the shows and movies your kids watch

and the video or computer games they play. Watch and play with them!

- Talk about what your kids are watching. TV and movies can spark interesting conversations that will help you and your children understand each other better.

Strategy #2: Family Night

If you want to take control of your home, start by setting aside one evening a week that your family spends together. That's not impossible, that's "doable." Choose one evening of the week and call it "Family Night." Our Family Night is Monday night.

Why have a family night? We have picked one night out of the week to get our kids away from the hustle and bustle that goes along with raising seven kids, running a business, and living in a busy urban area. It does not matter whether Family Night is Sunday, Monday, or Thursday, as long as the whole family knows that on a particular evening, no matter what is going on, it is the night for the family to get together.

Here is our Family Night schedule:

1. A moment of silence or prayer
2. Opening song
3. Values lesson
4. A role play
5. "Spotlight"
6. Closing song
7. Silence or prayer
8. Family Night treat

First, we find a place in the house where we can have some kind of order. Then we begin with a prayer. If prayer doesn't work for your family, have a moment of meditation or silence. Usually Brent or I will say the prayer, but we also give the kids a chance to lead the prayer. Then we sing a song together. The kids choose the song we will sing.

Singing together might sound corny, but there is something about voices blending and working together. Even if our harmony is off and we sing in different keys, singing makes us feel like we are able to accomplish things together. It also creates a joyous, fun feeling. (See ideas for songs and music on page 208.)

Next we have a lesson about values. Usually the parents present the lesson, but we also let the older kids give lessons.

Brent: *It's great to "turn the tables" and let a child be the teacher. Boy, they get real excited when no one is listening or someone is misbehaving. Phelecia and I help the kids learn how to get everyone's attention and keep it. The kids behave better after they have had to teach a lesson.*

For an example of a values lesson, we might talk about kindness. When we talk about being kind, we write "Be Kind" on a white board or large piece of paper. Then together we make a list of what everybody can do to be kind. We encourage them to do whatever they can to be kind and to secretly do one kind thing for somebody in the family or someone on the street during the coming week. We also ask the children to notice when others show kindness. The following week we ask, "Who saw someone being kind this week?" or "What did you do to be kind this week?" We give a "Kindness Award" to each person who witnessed or performed a kind act that week.

Here's another example of a values lesson. We feel that being of service to others is an important value. In regard to service, we discuss ways of making other people happy and serving other people. We talk about how you lose yourself in service and become a bigger and better person. Then we put this value into action with the help of the "Family Night Phantom." For example, we make cookies and secretly leave them at another family's front door. The idea is that the "Family Night Phantom" brings a treat or helps another family. (To help decide which values you want to teach, see Chapter 6.)

The Key to Teaching Good Decision-Making: Role Playing

After the lesson, we lead the kids in role-playing activities. During the role-playing part of Family Night, we put real-life situations in front of the kids, and play these situations out at home. Sometimes Brent or I take on a role or we ask the children to participate. Both ways are effective. Here are some real-life situations we have practiced:

- A "friend" tries to get someone to buy drugs, drink alcohol, or smoke.
- An adult tries to get a child to get in his car or go somewhere with him.
- A peer wants to shoplift, cut class, or plan a prank.
- Friends use crass or disrespectful language.

When similar situations have come up in real life, our children didn't say to themselves, "Oh no, what should I do? Which choice is right? Is the wrong choice *that* wrong?" Because we had practiced decision-making, our children knew the right answer.

Phelecia: *When my son was in kindergarten, a kid approached him in the school bathroom.*

"Hey, do you want to see my private parts?" the other kid said.

My son said, "No. I don't want to see your private parts, and I am going to go tell the teacher. That's not right."

And he ran and told the teacher.

When he got home, he was proud to say, "Mom, I did what we practiced!"

We try to use the role-playing part of Family Night wisely. We use this time to clearly tell our children how we feel about drugs, alcohol, and sex. We help them to understand when something *feels* right or wrong, it probably is. We go so far as to tell them what they should and shouldn't do! We understand that we cannot prepare for each and every tough situation in life. (The anxious parent inside of us is desperately saying, "But can't we try?") Rest assured, you can give your children the tools they need to make good decisions. Help them to practice making tough choices and to listen to their *own* feelings. This will give them the confidence to walk away from bad situations or just say, "No." *These decision-making skills will help them to be G-Rated citizens in an X-Rated world.*

In the "Spotlight"

Phelecia: *After the values lesson and role playing, we do what we call "Spotlight." I have a basket that contains a few things that the spotlight person likes. For instance I might say, "This person loves gummy worms and chocolate. This person is really good at playing with other kids in the family." After a few clues, the kids guess the name of the spotlight person. Then that person gets a treat from the basket. Plus, the child who is in the spotlight that week gets to go out with Dad.*

The spotlight part of Family Night is very special for our children. When a child is in the spotlight, each member of the family, in turn, tells something special and wonderful about him or her. To help the children think about ways to praise the person in the spotlight, we ask questions such as, "Why do you like this person?" "What makes this person special?" "Tell about something nice this person has done." The kids cannot wait for a turn to be in the spotlight, and so they look forward to Family Night.

Our children enjoy the compliments and praise received in the spotlight. To help them relive those wonderful feelings, sometimes we all write about the person and then read the comments aloud. If a child is too young to write, he or she dictates ideas to a parent or older child. When we choose to write about the special person, we all write on a small card like the one below. The person in the spotlight can carry this card and read it when a word of encouragement is needed. One of our daughters is in middle school, and she reports that reading good things about herself at school helps her if she is having a bad day.

Ashlyne: *After I was in the spotlight I felt really good about myself. I kept what my family had written and read it at school, and that made me feel good all over again.*

IN THE SPOTLIGHT: [NAME HERE]			
	What do you like about this person?	*What is special about this person?*	*This person did something wonderful. It was...*
Brent			
Phelecia			
Shane			
Chari			
Ashlyne			
McKay			
Dakota			
Saige			
Hunter			

Closing Activities

After the spotlight activity, we sing another song together, and then spend a moment in silence or prayer. Finally, there is the traditional Family Night treat. The child who was in the spotlight the week before chooses the treat and helps make it for the rest of the family.

Family Night Planning

To help you add Family Night to your routine, we have included a Family Night planning worksheet (see below). Make four copies of it, and use them to create four Family Nights that work for you and your children. There is also a section for evaluating each part of Family Night. At the end of one month, you'll have a new routine that includes a tried-and-true way for spending quality time with your family.

Family Night Activities	*Focus for this week:*	*The family member(s) in charge of these activities:*	*Evaluation of each Family Night Activity (e.g. "Was this successful?"):*
Moment of Silence/Prayer			
Opening Song			
Values Lesson			
Role Play			
"Spotlight"			
Closing Song			
Moment of Silence/Prayer			
Treat			

Avoiding Family Fight Night

Do not be afraid to vary the routine of Family Night. Go out with your family and play a round of miniature golf, go bowling, or ice-skating. You can start off by playing baseball together, or tennis, or football. Trying new activities is important, because Family Night can also turn into Family Fight Night. We joke about this sometimes. But that is part of being a family. Taking time to have fun as a family helps you get through the rough times.

Phelecia: *Family Night can be a tough time for teenagers. They might just lie on the floor like lumps. I remember loving Family Night as a teenager. But I never, ever said I liked it. I certainly didn't act as if I liked it.*

Teenagers will say, "Oh, I don't want to come to Family Night." But even if they just sit there and act like they are bored, they are listening. They are like sponges. They are taking in the songs, the lessons, and the love.

Brent: *It is never too late to start the tradition of Family Night. I can tell you right now if you don't practice anything else out of this book other than just doing this, it will still make a huge difference.*

Family Night is a time reserved for family to be together. That's it. It is one night a week when we sing and talk. If members of the family play an instrument, that's even better. It's a time to put other activities and worries aside and focus on the family. Remember, you can take control of your family. Start by taking control of one evening a week you spend together.

Strategy #3: The Family Report Card

Brent: *Our kids are graded constantly throughout their school years. The Family Report Card turns the tables. We, as parents, are going to be graded by our children. Don't get angry if the grades are not what you thought they should be. Respond with kindness and love.*

To make the Family Report Card easy for kids to understand, we created questions for them to answer. Questions such as, "Do I spend enough time with you?" "Are you proud of me as a parent?" "Do I keep my promises?" "Do I explain why I failed to keep my promises?" "Do I yell too much?" "Do I say, 'I'm sorry' enough?" "Do you feel loved unconditionally?" The Family Report Card on page 49 contains blank spaces so that you can tailor the report card to your family's needs.

The first time we asked our children to grade us using the Family Report Card, they gave us straight A's. We were upset, because we knew our kids were lying to us. Our children didn't want to hurt our feelings, so they gave us high grades for our parenting. We had to assure our children of two things:

1. That we wanted the truth.
2. That we would not get angry about their feelings or opinions.

Tell your children *and* show them that you will not get angry about the grades they give you. Use the Family Report Card in a non-threatening, loving way, and your children will feel safe giving you high and low grades.

Phelecia: *To make the Family Report Card work, we helped our children understand that we are aware of our own weaknesses, by giving examples of areas where Brent and I need to practice managing our emotions. Sometimes I raise my voice, and at times Brent has a "short fuse." We explained that we would grade ourselves lower in the area we call "Do I yell too much?" We* *asked them to use the report card to tell us about things we are doing that we are not aware of.*

After you use the Family Report Card for a while, you will realize, as we did, that "bad" grades are actually good! They mean your children feel free to communicate their true feelings. So think of the Family Report Card as a communication "icebreaker." It is a tool that opens up communication; it literally can break communication ice blocks between you and your children.

Brent: *Parents in my seminars sometimes say that they are afraid to use the Family Report Card. They are nervous about what their children might say about their parenting. Believe me, we have heard just about every possible criticism from our children. None of it has killed us, and we're better parents for it.*

After your children finish grading the Family Report Card, talk about why they chose the grades they did. Ask them for ways you can improve. At first, you may feel defensive or guilty when you hear your child's feelings. Choose not to be offended by criticism. Your children are just trying help you understand how they feel, what they mean, and what they need. It is a wonderful thing for a parent to know exactly what his or her child needs. Several years ago we learned that one of our children didn't feel loved. She wrote this on the report card. We felt terribly guilty at first. Then we focused on solving the problem. We found out what made her feel loved. We discovered ways to make her feel noticed, appreciated, and adored.

Brent: *As I mention in Chapter 7, my brother and I developed a communication tool called "The Hug Card." So I was dismayed when one of our kids gave me a "D" on the Family Report Card. He said he wanted more hugs. I felt that I hugged my kids all the time. My son felt that I hugged everyone else more than I hugged him. His perception was so different from my own.*

Get to Know Your Child

The results of the Family Report Card often remind Brent and me that we have no idea what our children are really thinking—they look at things differently from the way we do as parents. Yet, we want to have an open relationship with our children, and that means letting our guard down.

We have a favorite exercise we use when we hear, "You don't understand me!" A colleague developed a tool to ensure that you understand your child and, perhaps more importantly, to convince your child you are trying very hard to "get" who they are.

Here is how it works: Make two copies of the following questionnaire, one for you and one for your child. Answer the questions, and then share your answers. We guarantee that you and your children will learn a good deal about each other.

This exercise is not as easy as it first appears. Do not be surprised if you match only five or six answers. More than eight is great. If you want to know what motivates your children, you need to know their interests. This activity can help you understand more about your children. Repeat the activity with each of your children. You may also repeat the activity every few months. Make up your own questions. Many parents have told me that their children made a questionnaire for them. Have fun.

How well do you know your child?

Parents need to see things from their child's point of view. This includes knowing what your child is thinking about and what his or her interests are. We suggest answering each of the questions below the way you think your child would answer them. At the same time, have your child answer the questions. Compare answers.

1. My favorite TV show is________________________.
2. What I like best about myself is________________________.
3. My favorite thing to eat for dinner is________________________.
4. My favorite color is ________________________.
5. Other kids think I am________________________.
6. My favorite song is ________________________.
7. What I like best about my mother is ________________________.
8. My best school subject is ________________________.
9. My favorite video game is ________________________.
10. When I have to work around the house, I ________________________
    ________________________.
11. What I like best about my father is ________________________.
12. I like my teacher when ________________________.
13. My favorite movie is________________________.
14. I think my bedtime should be ________________________.
15. When I have free time, I like to________________________.
16. When I grow up, I want to ________________________.
17. I like people who ________________________.
18. What I would like to change about me is________________________.
19. I do not like people who________________________.
20. If I had lots of money, I would________________________.

Yes, it's scary to receive criticism from your children. The good news is that you will also have fewer regrets about your parenting if you are willing to hear and understand their feelings. When your kids are grown you will *not* have to say to yourself, "I wish I had known how my child felt. I would have done things differently." Try the Family Report Card and the How Well Do You Know Your Child? questionnaire and you will know how your children feel and you can respond accordingly.

We use the Family Report Card about once a month; that might be too often or not often enough for your needs. Use it in good times and especially during difficult times. Even if you only use it once a year, the important thing is that your family is communicating in a positive way.

FAMILY REPORT CARD™

Name ______________________ Name of Adult ______________________

Think about your parents or caregiver and give a letter grade, A-F, for each of the areas below.	Month 1	Month 2	Month 3	Month 4	Month 5	Month 6	Comments
1. Spends enough time with me.							
2. Listens to me.							
3. Responds to me in positive ways.							
4. Shows me he/she is proud of me.							
5. Keeps promises.							
6. Explains his/her actions to me (e.g. "I didn't keep my promise because…")							
7. Does not raise his/her voice or hit.							
8. Says, "I'm sorry" when necessary.							
9. Makes me feel loved.							
10. Hugs me.							
11. Other							

See the reverse side for instructions on how to grade the report card.

The Family Report Card is a communication tool to help your family express feelings. It's a simple, positive way to find out what your children are thinking.

Approach this activity without defensiveness. Your children might not give you the grades you want, but that is not important. Focus on the process itself—you are showing your child how to express feelings, desires, and opinions in a positive way. Ask your children how you can improve and respond with kindness and love.

If your family discovers that there are many areas that need work, choose one area and then identify one specific thing you can change and implement it. In a month, go through this process again and choose another area that needs work. Don't forget to applaud yourself for things that have improved.

How to Use the Family Report Card

Read the entire Family Report Card with your child or teen. Explain that for each area of your relationship you would like to be given a letter grade, A-F. Discuss one or two of the topics on the card. For example, "Spends enough time with me." Discuss the topic and let everyone express their feelings and opinions. Talk about the grades and what each letter grade stands for and ask them to complete the report card. There is a blank space for personalizing the report card.

A = Excellent

B = Good, above average

C = Average

D = Not so good, below average

F = Terrible! This is an area to work on. Focus on specific actions for improvement and re-evaluate in a month.

Strategy #4: The Band-Aid Magnet

When children fall down and get a cut, they come running to a parent so he or she can "make it all better" with a bandage. When children get their feelings hurt, sometimes they do not have the courage to say they are hurt. That is where the Band-Aid Magnet comes in handy.

As you can see from the illustration below, a Band-Aid Magnet is a magnetic sheet with a picture of a band-aid on it. Turn to page 223 to order a magnet for each member of your family, both children and adults. Write each family member's name in the space provided. We keep all the magnets on the side of the refrigerator, where they are out of sight but even the smallest can reach them. You could also put them on the front at the bottom if the sides of your fridge are not accessible. If you would like, line them up in order from oldest to youngest. Then, if a family member has hurt feelings, he or she moves the magnet to front or the top of the fridge. The other family members will notice that one of the magnets is out of place or is at the top of the fridge, and it is their job to find out what that person is feeling.

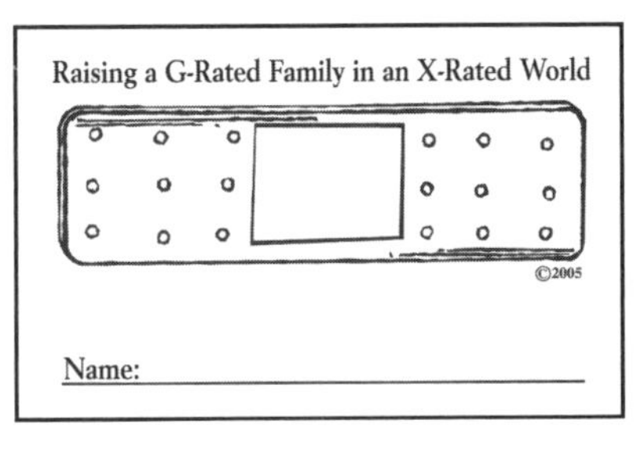

Brent: *The first day we had the magnets on the fridge, I assumed that they would be something our younger kids would enjoy and use. To my surprise, I found that my teenage son and my wife, Phelecia, had moved their magnets to the front of the refrigerator.*

The Band-Aid Magnet has helped our family deal with small emotional upsets before they become big ones. One day our son put his magnet up because he felt Brent treated him unfairly. The two talked about it and both felt better. Phelecia put her magnet up because she felt that no one was helping her with household chores. We all pitched in and Phelecia felt listened to. Younger kids like the Band-Aid Magnet because they don't have to find the words right away to describe their feelings. Older kids like it because they don't have to feel embarrassed about revealing how they feel. The Band-Aid Magnet is a nonverbal tool for helping families communicate.

How will these strategies help you raise G-Rated kids? We believe that children who are raised with appropriate limits and solid parenting are more self-confident and secure. These children become adults who turn away from negative behaviors such as abusing drugs, alcohol, or sex. And these are children who turn to their parents (or just folks who will listen to them) for advice or help.

In the next chapter, we focus on communication skills—the "how-tos" of respectful listening and speaking.

Chapter 4

"Please Just Listen to Me!": Develop and Use Good Communication Skills

***Brent:** I was preparing for a motivational parenting rally back in Maryland and going over what I wanted to say to the participants. Part of what I planned to talk about was how I spend time communicating with my kids. About that time, my son came up to me and said, "Hey, Dad, let's get going. You said you would play ball with me." I told him, "You know, I am very busy right now, and I just don't have time. Give me five more minutes."*

Five minutes later, he came back, but I was still going over my speech. He said, "Come on, Dad. Let's go play ball. Come on." Well, I put him off again.

Moments later, I saw a baseball coming toward me at a high rate of speed. It missed my head by about a foot and bounced off the wall.

A Wake-Up Call

The truth is, sometimes we hear what our children are saying, but we don't really listen. Our son later told us that he felt ignored, so he threw the baseball to get Brent's attention. Clearly, this was not a moment of perfect parenting. But being a perfect parent is not important. We are not perfect parents, but we try to be aware when our children send strong messages and we try to make changes accordingly.

Brent: *I got the message my son sent with the baseball. There I was, preparing to go and talk to parents on how to communicate with their kids; yet, I had a son who was trying to communicate with me, and I was pushing him away. That kind of woke me up. I put my speech down, and we went out and played for about an hour or so. That meant everything to my son.*

Communication Idea Box

Feelings Are Okay, Violence Is Not

Help children deal with anger by giving them outlets for the feeling:

- Encourage young children to find an adult to help mediate the dispute.
- Take a walk or a run together.
- Provide a punching bag to work out feelings.
- Encourage the child/teen to leave the room for a moment.
- Teach a little rhyme, "When enraged, disengage."

The baseball-throwing story illustrates that listening is an important communication skill. When we really listen to a child we are modeling respect for his or her feelings, thoughts, and experiences.

Adele Faber and Elaine Mazlish are experts on communication. In their book *How to Talk So Kids Will Listen & Listen So Kids Will Talk,* the authors give parents four ways to be better listeners:

1. Listen quietly and attentively.
2. Acknowledge their feelings with a word. "Oh…Mmm…really?…I see…what else?…"
3. Give the feeling a name. "That sounds embarrassing?" "How frustrating!" "That made you angry."
4. Give the child his wishes in a fantasy. "I wish I could make your favorite cereal appear right now!"[25]

The authors do not suggest that parents do anything complicated while listening. Don't try to solve the problem for the child. Don't analyze the root causes of the issue, deny the feelings, or give advice. Just listen.

Communication Idea Box

Use Magic Wands and Fairy Dust with Younger Children

When you pretend to have a magic wand or fairy dust and make something magically happen for your young child, you are validating the child's desires. You are also demonstrating, in a silly way, that the child can't always get what he wants when he wants it. This response adds humor to a situation that can be very difficult for parents and young children to handle.

Life today is so busy; the difficult part about communicating with our children is finding the time to really listen. With seven children, we often find ourselves listening to our children as we make dinner, pay bills, or fold laundry. But we can still listen and listen well. We have found that if we make eye contact and give neutral responses such as "oh," "mmmm," "really," or "I see," our children will continue to talk. Our motto is: listen early and often!

Communication Idea Box

Six Things You Should Never Say to Your Child

1. "You sound like your mother."
2. "Where did you come up with that idea?"
3. "I can't understand why you would do that."
4. "You never say anything positive. Why are you so miserable?"
5. "You always have to have it your way."
6. "That is your father's fault." "Your mother doesn't know what she is talking about."

Communication Idea Box
Four Things Parents Should Never Say to Each Other in Front of a Child
1. "You have never been able to handle her. You always let her get away with that."
2. "What are you going to do about that?"
3. "I don't care what you do. You always do what you want to do with him anyway."
4. "He's your son, you deal with it. He's stubborn, just like you."

Fostering Communication

When children or adults are given the chance to talk about a feeling or experience without worrying about the judgment of the listener, an answer or resolution to the situation often reveals itself. Here are some phrases to use when listening to your child that show you are listening and interested, but that do not express judgment. In the left-hand column are comments we often want to make, but that close down communication between parent and child. On the right are responses that foster better communication.

Communication Idea Box	
When you want to say:	***A better response would be:***
"Oh, honey, don't get so upset!"	"You have strong feelings about this."
"That's life, dear, it's best to get over it."	"It sounds like you were embarrassed and humiliated by what happened."
"I can't get that for you and that's final!"	"If I had a glittering magic wand, I would make that appear like this, 'poof!'" or "I wish I could sprinkle fairy dust on your homework so it would be done in one minute!"
"Well, I would have done things differently in that situation. Next time you should…"	"Really?" "Go on, tell me more." "Hmmm…" "Wow!" "I see."

All of the "better" responses have certain characteristics. Some rephrase what the child or teenager has said to make certain we understand. Other responses are open-ended so that the child will continue to talk. The tone of each response is not critical, and all responses are an attempt to hear more than what is being said. They serve as a guide to help the child or teenager say more.

When you are listening to your child, think of responses that help you "listen between the lines":

- Clarify what is said.
- Continue the conversation with open-ended questions.
- Cut-out all advice, criticism, or judgment.

When parents are good listeners, it builds trust and creates warmth between parent and child. When your child has ample time to express herself, she may be able to better understand her feelings and be less afraid of negative ones. She'll also be better equipped to communicate well with others.

Communication Idea Box

Hang Up and Listen!

It's great that cellular phones allow us to communicate whenever and where ever, but it's sad the way some parents ignore their children and talk on the cell phone instead.

We urge parents to hang up or turn off the cell phone when picking up or dropping off kids at school, camp, or a friend's house—at any transition point when a parent is taking leave of or picking up a child. At these moments, take time to focus on your child. Give a hug or kiss goodbye or hello. Allow them to tell you what has happened during the day. The stories they tell you give you clues about what is important to them. Let your actions show your children they are special and that you feel they warrant your undivided attention.

Build Trust and a Successful Teenager

Phelecia: *My conversations with my children have changed so much over the years. You know, I have a son in high school now, and he used to talk to me about airplanes or baseball. Now he talks to me about real-life problems.*

Recently he said to me, "Mom, since I have been a freshman in high school, do you know how many times I have been offered drugs?" Of course, inside I was shaking, but I kept my composure and said, "No, how many?"

"Four times."

"Well, what did you say?"

"I told them, 'No, I don't do that.'"

"Well, what did the other kids say then?"

"Well most of them said, 'Wow! You're good. I wish I could be as good as that.'"

I praised my son for coming to me and letting me know. I felt really honored that he and I have the kind of relationship that he felt he could come to me with things like that.

He still comes to me with personal issues or about different things at school, asking questions like, "What do you think about that?" Recently, he told me about a girl he knows who said something inappropriate. He said to me, "I felt really bad when she said that, Mom, and I wanted to let you know that. That was wrong, what she said." It's so important to be interested in what our children are saying.

Listening to your children is a small action that has far-reaching consequences. According to Dr. Sal Severe, a school psychologist with over 25 years of experience counseling children and teenagers, troubled teenagers and successful teenagers describe their ability to talk to parents very differently. Dr. Severe says that troubled teenagers say, "I can't talk to my parents. They don't understand me. They don't know anything about me. I don't trust them. They don't trust me." In contrast, successful teenagers describe their parents as good listeners who they can talk to and with whom there is mutual trust.

Why do children and teenagers need to trust their parents? So that when they have a problem they can go to their parents for help. Without their parents' help, they face problems alone. Some children and teenagers find this independence scary and painful. They try to escape their loneliness and problems by turning to drugs, drinking, gangs, and even suicide. Communication is extremely important for raising G-Rated children in an X-Rated world.

Listen Carefully

Build trust by listening respectfully to your child and showing a sincere interest in what he or she has to say. Here are some ideas for respectful communication:

Communication Idea Box
Phrases and Comments that Demonstrate Respect and Foster Trust:
"I noticed that you said/did/ ________. Can you tell me about that?"
"I may not have listened well the last time we talked. I'm sorry. If you will give me another chance, I'd like to listen now."
"I would like to hear what you think."
"I trust your ideas on…"
"I may not agree with you, but it's good to say what you feel."

Try to listen for the feelings behind the words your child is saying—or perhaps shouting. We received the following story via e-mail from a mother who successfully used this strategy with her eight-year-old boy.

My son's two best friends live on our street and the three boys play together daily. Late one summer afternoon my son, Everett, charged into the house with a red face and teary eyes. "I hate Owen and Connor so much. I always help Owen get his Pokemon to higher levels and then he tells Connor he did it himself. He is such a liar! And now Owen's father says we have to go to the pool to swim. He just wants us to stop playing Gameboy. Mom, Owen's dad is forcing us to go to the pool!" Everett stomped to his room and "bang" went the door. Moments later he emerged in his swim trunks and yelled, "Mom, where are my swim goggles?" I triumpantly produced the goggles and a beach towel when Everett screeched, "Mom! Owen's dad is driving Owen and Connor to the pool. We need to hurry!" I calmly asked why we were going to the pool if he didn't want to go. "Mom! Stop wasting time. I'll miss the pool!"

Inside, I was seething at his rudeness and confused by his intense anger. But I reminded myself to "hear the feelings behind the words." I had a sense that something was going on between Everett and his friends, so I decided to patiently take Everett and his sister to the pool to see what was really going on.

As we pulled out of the driveway, Everett said sadly, "Connor and Owen went to see a movie and they didn't invite me. They always do that. They go off and do fun things without me and then tell me about it. Then they invite me to do dumb stuff like swimming." In my head I was recounting all the places the boys had been to in the last two weeks: Chuck E. Cheese's; the water park; the Seal Sanctuary; the beach; the "paint-it-yourself" ceramics studio. In spite of all he and his friends did together, Everett felt excluded if Owen and Connor did anything *without him. I said to Everett, "Does it make you sad when Owen talks about things he did with Connor and not you?" He started to cry, "Why does Owen do that? He always brags about what he does with Connor."*

Because Everett's mother was able to "hear the feelings behind the words," she could validate his feelings and give him some wisdom about friendships and sharing feelings.

When our children are screaming, crying, or angry, effective communication can be difficult or even impossible. Rest assured, at times we all say the wrong thing and model ineffective communication strategies for our children, but if we practice listening for the feelings that are motivating what is said, we will create closer bonds with our children.

Phelecia: *One day, our son was enraged with Brent and said mean and hurtful things about him. My son is usually not like that, so I was extremely shocked. But instead of getting mad at him for saying terrible things, I knew I needed to hear the feelings behind the words he was saying.*

Calmly, I asked him to talk to me alone. We were able to share our feelings, and he was able to open up and tell me why he was feeling the way he was. This was such a beautiful experience, communicating effectively, because I was able to listen to the words behind the walls and hear what he wanted on the other side.

He simply needed to hear that he was loved, that he was not bad, and that his father didn't mean to embarrass or hurt him. Sometimes we have to listen to what our children are saying behind the words—especially words spoken in anger and pain.

When you and your kids yell at each other or communication breaks down, take time to analyze what went wrong. Let the bad situation become a learning moment. Apologize to your child and vow to try and do a better job next time.

Go Where They Are

Brent: *Our eight-year-old boy is really into bugs. I mean, bugs are his life. He can spend hours and hours looking at one bug. One day, I remember yelling out to him in the backyard to go clean up. "I need the backyard cleaned up. Son, can you go do this?" But it was like nothing was penetrating through his brain. He didn't hear me. He didn't want to hear me, and I wasn't getting through to him.*

So I went out to the backyard and I lay on the ground. My son didn't look at me. He just kept looking at the bugs, as if I was not even lying next to him. I started talking to the bugs, and then I said, "This bug said he wants you to put him away so you can clean up."

It was like a light flashed in his head. He looked at me and said, "What does he want me to do?" "He wants you to put him away. He wants you to put him with his mommy so he can go eat dinner, and so that you can help me."

The response I got from my son was unbelievable. He put the bug in a safe place and started cleaning the backyard. To get that response, I took something that interested him, got down on his level, and the communication lines were blasted open.

Sometimes we have to meet children more than halfway to communicate effectively with them. This story is a good example. When a child is not listening or responding, parents often begin repeating themselves or, eventually, yelling. In our experience, neither works. Meeting the child at his or her level does work—just as it did in this example with Dakota and the bugs.

Parents naturally use different communication strategies with children depending on age and personality. A friend of ours has a creative strategy she related to us:

My daughter Brita loves to write. When she becomes crabby, sulky, or when we can just tell something is on her mind, we write her a little note to ask what is going on. She writes back and that's how we can learn her feelings and how we might help. Now that we have multiple computers at our home, we even send e-mails back and forth to each other. I believe she feels safer and more willing to open up when she writes.

Another friend related this story about his son:

Our son Evan, who is 14, will share his feelings and thoughts, but only when he is doing something. To engage him in conversation, we first engage him in an activity, and that can be anything: playing catch, taking a walk, washing the car, cleaning his room—anything that he needs or wants to do. Typically, he will begin to share his thoughts and experiences during these times.

Communication Idea Box
We have found, as our children enter the teenage years, a strategy of "talking and walking" really works. Many teens need an activity to "camouflage" their need to talk. First, engage your teen in an activity, then engage him in conversation.

Since we have seven children, we have lots of experience with children and teenagers of different personalities and temperaments. We have learned that there is no one best place or time to discuss feelings and thoughts with our children. We simply observe each child to discover the best time and place to talk with that child. Our goal is to establish good communication patterns so when *big* stuff comes up, our kids will turn to us.

Communication Red Flags

As you observe your children and teens, watch for "red flags." One important warning sign for problems is a sudden and extreme change in behavior, as the following story illustrates.

Phelecia: *A good friend of mine is a stay-at-home mom who supervises her son consistently and carefully. At ten years old, he* *was well-behaved and got good grades—a model child. Each day after finishing his homework, he went next door to play. Although the neighbor boy's parents were not home, my friend was able to see her son there through the kitchen window, and she would wave at him now and again.*

Suddenly, her ten-year-old's behavior changed. As soon as he came home, he would throw his books down, refuse to do his homework, and angrily run next door. About this time the school principal called my friend in and reported changes in her son's behavior at school. "We thought we should bring it to your attention," the principal said.

My friend and her husband got help from a psychologist. Come to find out, while their son was playing over at the neighbor's house, he and his friend, with the aid of an older brother, were downloading hardcore pornography. Their son became addicted to the pornography he was exposed to at this friend's house. It took a long time and a lot of therapy to help him get his life back.

Even if we think we are supervising our children, we need to watch for red flags. We need to pay attention to behavior changes and take steps to find out what is causing the change in behavior.

Open the Door to Communication

Phelecia: *It may not be an original idea, but I make a point to ask our children "How was your day?" after school. Or, in the morning, I ask, "How was your night?" Of course, sometimes when you ask a child about what happened in school, you'll get the standard non-answer, "Nothing." In those cases, be more creative by asking, "What new thing did you learn in school today?" or "What do you like most about your art assignment?" or "What was the funniest thing that happened at school today?" If your child is grumpy in the morning, maybe all you need to say is, "It's so good to see you this morning." I try to open the door to communication, and make my children feel loved and let them* *know I really care how they feel. The message to them is, "I'm ready to listen when you're ready to talk."*

Keeping lines of communication open with children is difficult, but even more challenging when they misbehave. Even when a situation is negative, though, you can respond positively and keep talking.

Brent: *Our six-year-old daughter wanted to go play with a next-door neighbor. I told her she could later, but not right then because we were doing something as a family. A few minutes later, I looked outside and there was my daughter playing with her little friend. I went outside and let her know it wasn't okay for her to disobey. I told her to sit on her bed for five minutes and think about what she should have done. She thought about it and told me that next time she would obey us.*

When kids don't do as they are told, definitely keep your cool, but let them know where you stand so they learn right from wrong.

We accept that our children will make mistakes, and when it happens, we clearly state what went wrong and let the child know what was okay and what was not. It is also important to ask children to reflect on their behavior and have them say what they would do differently. Your kids might make the same mistake again, but you are teaching them to think about their behavior and helping them to become thoughtful, conscious adults.

We also want our children to have proper self-esteem because children who feel good about themselves tend to avoid what we consider X-Rated things, like drugs, violence, and sexual promiscuity. To help develop good self-esteem, when our children misbehave, we focus on the behavior rather than the child's character. We find it helpful to say:

> "That is not okay. I don't want you to [describe what was done]. I need you to help me fix/repair/clean up."

By saying "that is not okay," we make it clear that the behavior is unacceptable. However, we do not say that the child is bad, naughty, mean, or any other adjective that insults the child's character.

We use statements that begin with "I." When you start a sentence with "I," you are less likely to blame or insult the child. Instead, you are more likely to express how you feel about a situation. That authentic response helps the child understand how his actions make others feel. It also allows you to vent your feelings appropriately, so that you don't keep them bottled up only to explode later.

Communication Idea Box
Tips for Reacting Positively, Even in Negative Situations
Say, "That is not okay."
Focus on the child's behavior, not the child's character.
Use statements that begin with "I."
Ask:
"What did you do?"
"What were you supposed to do?" OR "What is the rule?"
"Did you make the right choice?" OR "Was that a good decision?"
"What could you have done differently?"
"What could you do next time?"

Teaching Instead of Punishing

A negative situation can be made more positive when parents use the situation to help the child make a better decision in the future. The following questioning technique, developed by Dr. Sal Severe, will allow you to guide your child/teen's thinking after he or she has made a mistake or is trying to make a decision:[26]

When our children make poor decisions, we can ask the right questions to avoid arguments and help them make better decisions in the future.

But what about dealing with a child who does not want to listen or talk? The following exchange illustrates how to use Dr. Severe's questioning technique with a strong-willed child who has made a mistake and is unwilling to cooperate.

Mom: "What happened, Jake?"

Jake: "Nothing happened."

Mom: "What did you do?"

Jake: "I said nothing happened."

Mom: "It looks to me like you hit your brother."

Jake: "Then why did you ask if you already know?"

Mom: "We have spoken about this before. I know you had strong feelings, but it's not okay to hit. Let's work together so that the next time this happens you can make a better decision. We can decide what to do about this later."

Notice that Mom understood that Jake was not willing to cooperate but she stayed positive and calm. She did not lecture Jake about not hitting and she did not insult his character by calling him mean or stubborn. Mom also realized Jake was not willing to talk and appropriately delayed any further discussion until Jake calmed down. She also assured Jake that together they would help him control his feelings and make a better decision next time.[27]

Strive for Progress, Not Perfection

There are simple, almost commonsense things to keep in mind while developing good communication between family members. For example, don't yell! Yelling makes kids feel awful and doesn't accomplish what you started out to do, unless you just want to humiliate and upset each other.

***Brent and Phelecia:** We are not perfect. Brent has a yelling problem. It's something he's been working on for more than 16 years; he's gained a lot more control. Phelecia, on the other hand, is not a yeller (for which Brent is grateful). If somebody in the family spills the milk at breakfast, Phelecia would be likely to say, "I'm sorry that happened. Everyone makes mistakes. Okay, help me clean up the milk. We will clean it up together." And how much more productive that is for everybody! The milk gets cleaned up and everyone goes to school and work with a better attitude.*

If you have a "yeller" in the family, however, the morning could go very differently. The yeller yells, "Why did you spill this milk?" The person who spilled the milk feels like a loser. The rest of the family feels stressed, too, and the day starts off badly.

Is the glass of milk worth feelings like that? We don't think so. That's why we suggest that fellow yellers might have to "take ten" in situations like this. Walk out of the room calmly and without slamming doors, count to ten, and then come back in.

Finally, don't ever be afraid to say "I'm sorry" to your children. As adults, we sometimes believe that we are always right and that we know it all, but we don't. So when we've done something wrong, we need to go to our children and say, "You know, honey, I'm very sorry. Dad was wrong. I should not have yelled at you." Some parents worry that admitting failure will make them weak, but it's just the opposite! We all make mistakes. Nobody is perfect. If you are willing to show your children that you make mistakes, too, and are willing to say you're sorry, that's a wonderful gift. Not only do you teach them that it's okay not to be perfect, you teach them to admit when they're wrong. You teach them to apologize to others. And you build another level of trust among yourselves.

Communication Idea Box
Good Communication: The Basics
Listen attentively and without judgment, advice, or criticism.
Respond with open-ended questions that encourage more talking.
Ask questions that clarify what has been said.
Validate feelings, wishes, and desires.
Use statements that begin with "I."
When a child misbehaves, focus on the behavior, not on character.
Let your child/teenager calm down if he/she is not ready to talk or listen.

If you are having trouble talking or listening to your kids, copy the chart above and tape it to your refrigerator. These basic skills will help.

Brent and I believe that parents who model good communication skills can raise G-Rated kids in an X-Rated world. We want our children to listen to us and to talk with us. This exchange of ideas and feelings brings us closer, and provides the emotional intimacy that enriches human relationships. Children who have learned to communicate well and have formed strong bonds within the family will seek out similar healthy relationships as they enter the real world. Our hope is that they will reject relationships that are shallow or exploitive—those types of relationships that are so often portrayed on television, in movies, and in music videos. Good communication skills help establish and sustain relationships.

What about when we discipline our children? Parents often feel that lines of communication close down at times when they have to set limits. Do you want to keep communicating with your children and teach them self-discipline? In the next chapter, we will explore ways parents can keep lines of communication open by using specific discipline techniques.

Chapter 5

"Think Again!": Discipline in the G-Rated World

***Brent:** I was outside a neighbor's house having a good chat, and my oldest son was nearby playing with a huge rubber snake. He was flicking the snake back and forth like a whip. I told him three or four times to stop because I knew the snake was going to hit me.*

I was right.

Moments later, I felt an intense, stinging sensation on my neck. My son took off, and as he ran by our house, he yelled to Phelecia, "Dad is going to kill me."

My son was right. In that moment, I felt like I wanted to kill him, although I would never do such a thing.

When it comes to discipline, we accept that our children will not always cooperate, and that we will not be perfect parents. Each day we strive for progress, not perfection. By reading this book, you have also taken the first step to becoming a better parent. You've found the courage to learn different parenting strategies. Now you need to make two promises to yourself.

Promise #1: Be Patient with Yourself and Your Kids.

***Brent:** I tell parents in seminars, "If you have had a bratty kid for eight years, it's going to take some time for you both to change. Be patient."*

Promise #2: Practice New Parenting Tips.

We have seven kids and lots of parenting experience, but we get tested just like you. Take the rubber snake story. We are able to joke with our son about it now, but at the time, it was pretty serious. Looking back, we realize that it would have been better to have walked over to our son and respectfully taken the snake away. The child was not listening, so asking was not working.

Defining "Good" Discipline

A big part of raising G-Rated kids is teaching them self-control through discipline and limits. Some parents have a hard time disciplining their children. It is easy to say what good discipline is, but it can be hard to follow through. It gets even more challenging when parents are tired and busy, or when kids are cranky and asserting their independence or just plain misbehaving. Keep this thought in mind when you are struggling with discipline issues:

> **Your children want discipline. They want you to tell them what to do. They want boundaries and limits because these things make children feel guided and loved.**

Good discipline techniques show your children you care about them and want them to succeed in the world. Children do not like to feel out of control. But without discipline, children can certainly feel that way. Discipline is a great and positive tool. Change your attitude about it. Instead of feeling that teaching discipline is a burden and difficult, recognize that it is a way to show your children you love them.

Is Spanking Good Discipline?

Brent: *As young parents, Phelecia and I believed in spanking, but we've come to realize it's a short-term answer to the long-term* *issue of discipline. Spanking didn't solve anything for us. Most of the time, my emotions got the best of me, and I spanked the kids harder than I should have because I was working out my own anger. The parents that I know who spank admit that they have lost control at times and have spanked their kids more than they would have liked.*

Our discussion of "good" discipline starts with spanking because everyone has opinions and feelings about it. Psychologists and child development specialists have ideas about it. Your parents and relatives have probably told you their thoughts on it. Frankly, we have changed from spanking to *not spanking*. Instead, we define good discipline as guidance.

Discipline Is Guiding

The goal of discipline is to guide your children in the right direction. Proper discipline does not belittle children, and it does not include yelling, shouting, demanding, or spanking. These things only create angry, resentful, and rebellious children. Discipline is a tool that helps children develop self-control, so that when a parent is *not* around, these children will make good choices.

Phelecia: *It is important to discipline with love. I don't think spanking is the way to go because it creates more and more anger. With spanking, it seems you have to up the ante higher and higher, until spanking almost becomes child abuse. That is not productive at all for you or the child.*

Brent: *I got spanked as a child, and it didn't affect me psychologically. I didn't like to get spanked, but I would rather have gotten a spanking than a "time out," because when the spanking was done, it was all over and I could go and play and have a good time. I did not learn much from getting spanked. I feel it is more effective to sit down and talk with your child about his or her behavior and what you expect.*

One goal of our discipline techniques is to get our kids to "think again." We want them to be aware of their actions and think about what they are doing. To reach this goal, it is helpful to understand how children learn.

How Children Learn

If you want well-behaved children, start by looking at your own behavior. Child psychologist Dr. Sal Severe has this to say about how children learn:

> Children learn by copying. A child's potential to observe and imitate is a remarkable quality. Scientists refer to this as modeling...Children learn attitudes, values, personal preferences, and even some habits by modeling...Think carefully about your behavior. What you say and do in front of your children influences their thinking and behavior. You are their model.[28]

Brent: *Phelecia and I were cleaning the kitchen one evening, when our two-year-old daughter and her four-year-old brother ran in shouting, "Come quick and see what we made!"*

The kids proudly showed us that they had decorated the sofas and carpet with three gallons of cotton-candy sugar. We saw the mess and the two innocent, creative children and had to laugh. Then we taught them both how to use the vacuum cleaner.

We all learned something from this mess. As parents, we learned the importance of avoiding trouble by keeping some things out of reach. But the children, as young as they were, learned something as well. They learned that Mom and Dad would not scream and yell if the kids misbehave. Your reaction to misbehavior speaks volumes, so keep your volume down! If you want your kids to come to you with serious problems when they are older, then try to keep your cool when they act up as children.

We have found that natural consequences help children control their behavior, but also keep the lines of communication open. In the case of the cotton-candy sugar, we all had to clean up the mess. We like to think that this natural consequence will help them learn not to do this again, but we understand that raising kids is a messy business.

Finally, our reaction to the "cotton-candy mess" modeled patience and guidance for our children. If you want your kids to yell, complain, whine, and nag, then go ahead and model yelling and nagging. If you want your kids to be thoughtful and look for solutions to problems, then respond to misbehavior firmly but gently with thoughtful solutions.

If your child's behavior concerns you, look closely at your behavior. Children learn what they live. When they live with responsible parents, they become responsible children. They will grow up to be responsible parents to your grandchildren. You have an obligation to be the best model that you can be. Your children do as you do.

Teach Your Kids Self-Discipline

To teach your children self-discipline, we suggest that you watch your own behavior *and* give your children choices. We have already discussed why your own behavior is important, but how do appropriate choices help parents raise G-Rated kids? Choices help children see that you value their thoughts and opinions. Giving your children choices shows them that you are fair and gives children a chance to practice making decisions without the consequences being too serious.

Here is what Dr. Severe says about giving children choices:

> Think about your child's choices, rules, and activities in three ways. Some things are required: earning passing grades, working around the house. Some things you will negotiate: curfew, TV programs, family dress code,

> make-up, and snacks. Give them full authority in some choices: sports, music lessons (which instrument he/she will play), school activities. As children mature and show more responsibility, gradually allow them more authority over their lives. If you expect more responsibility from your older children, give them more privileges. "You are three years older, I expect more from you." Higher expectations need a higher incentive. Allow older children a later bedtime, more allowance, and more activities. This encourages them to continue to behave responsibly and make good choices. It gives them confidence.[29]

A close friend gave us a great idea for incorporating choices into our disciplining strategies. It is called a parent-child contract, and it helps older and some younger kids learn self-discipline by making choices. Here's how we use this strategy:

> As parents, we decide what we would like our oldest son to do. Then, we sign a contract with him, and *we let him choose the consequences if he does not hold up his end of the deal.* For example, if he doesn't abide by the rules, then he can't go to his friend's house or go out on the weekends. The point is that our son helps decide what the rules are—within reason, of course.

Phelecia: *We all talk about the responsibilities and consequences before we sign the parent-child contract, just like a real contract. My son knows ahead of time the consequences if he doesn't do the things that he said that he would, because he chose the consequences himself.*

This kind of contract is great because it lets children decide their own consequences for breaking rules. Brent and I were surprised to find that they could be pretty harsh on themselves.

Another Self-Discipline Tool: Charts

If you feel your child is too young for a parent-child contract, a behavior and chore chart might be the answer. Charts work best for children up to age 12.

A posted chart becomes a visual reminder to be consistent. Charts prompt you to look for good behavior. They provide positive interactions between you and your children. They promote a healthy family climate. They encourage everyone to work together. Charts furnish both parents with an identical strategy. This increases consistency between parents.

Use a chart to reinforce good behavior and promote helping around the house. Identify the priority behaviors and chores you want to increase. List each behavior and chore on the chart. When your child behaves or completes a chore, put a smile in the box. At the end of the day, add up the number of happy faces.

Points, check marks, plus signs, or stickers work equally well. Awards on the chart are enough to satisfy some children. They do not always need other incentives. However, some children need stronger incentives.

Here's how charts work:

> Trade smiles (or whatever mark you use) for a reward or incentive. Each smile face could be worth a minute or two of extra story time, game time, or play time before going to bed. Some children like a reward each day plus a bonus activity for having a good week. Each smile could be worth game time at the end of the day. Total the smiles for the week. For example, having a friend spend the night costs 15 smiles. Be flexible. Do what works best with your children.

Jenny's Chart (☺ = two extra minutes of story time)							
Behavior	***Mon***	***Tue***	***Wed***	***Thur***	***Fri***	***Sat***	***Sun***
Shares her toys	☺ ☺	☺ ☺ ☺	☺ ☺ ☺	☺ ☺ ☺ ☺	☺ ☺ ☺	☺ ☺ ☺	☺ ☺ ☺ ☺
Listens the first time	☺ ☺ ☺ ☺	☺ ☺	☺ ☺ ☺	☺ ☺ ☺	☺ ☺ ☺ ☺	☺ ☺ ☺	☺ ☺ ☺
Daily Total	**6**	**5**	**6**	**7**	**7**	**6**	**7**
Weekly Total	**44**						

Always accompany an incentive with an encouraging statement. It is important to earn a reward. It is more important to develop a sense of responsibility. Aim for self-reward. "You had a great week. I am glad Trina can spend the night. I hope you feel proud of yourself."

Select behaviors that increase the chances of success. Do not load the chart with troublesome misbehaviors. Your child will see the chart as impossible. Choose some behaviors and chores that are easy and fun. You can also change the behaviors and chores. You may have a list of eight or more priorities. Rotate two or three of these each week. This keeps things interesting.

Have a section for bonus points. Anytime your child does something extra, helpful, or kind, add a smile. When you see special effort, add a smile. Children respond favorably to this technique. You can use a chart to improve a child's attitude. For example, if the behavior is "Craig will talk politely to his sister," each time that Craig is polite to his sister, catch him. Put a smile on his chart. Tell him you appreciate his politeness.

Develop charts for a week at a time. You may choose a five-, six-, or seven-day week. Some parents only use charts during the busy work week. Some parents use the chart seven days a week to provide a high level of consistency. Do what works for your family. Some parents use laminated tag board and an erasable marker. That way the chart can be reused each week. Some parents draw a grid on a sheet of paper and make several photocopies. Some parents create the chart on a computer. They can make changes and print a new version each week.

Develop charts with your children. Dual participation causes children to have ownership in the chart. Let your children draw designs and color the chart. Let them suggest some of the behaviors and incentives. Involvement creates interest and motivation.

You can use charts to redirect a child who is beginning to misbehave. For example:

> *Alex, I want you to see something before you get into trouble. Look at your chart. Look how well you have been listening. Look how you have improved. I know you feel proud about yourself. I know you can make a better decision. I know you can behave.*

Here is the wrong way:

> *I don't know why you can't behave for more than three days. This chart is supposed to make you behave.*

Charts help you avoid arguments. Written expectations and consequences permit no leeway for misinterpretation. Your children can see what they have or have not done. Charts teach responsibility. Charts show children how they are doing. Charts give children feedback about their behavior. When your child is doing well, a chart shows progress. This creates feelings of success and increases motivation. When your child is not doing well, a chart will show the exact behaviors he needs to improve. You and your child can concentrate on the behaviors that need work.[30]

Reward Good Behavior

Stickers or happy faces give children immediate rewards for good behavior. Eventually, you want your children to work for a few days or a week before receiving a reward. Begin with rewards at the end of each day, then after two days, etc.

Incentives for Children Who are Under 12 Years Old	*Incentives for Children 12 and Older (This list may include the list for younger children as well.)*
Hugs and kisses/praise and encouragement	Compliments
Complimenting your child in front of others	Activities with friends/Going to the mall/shopping
Using the computer to play games	Computer time/on-line account
One-on-one time with a parent	New clothes
Brother's Day/ Sister's Day	Cosmetics/hair styled
A special day with a parent	Snacks
Roughhousing with a parent	Money/allowance/doing work for money
Surprises	Having a friend over for lunch/dinner
Back/foot rubs	Choosing an activity for the family
Thank you notes in lunch box	Time alone/being allowed to do things alone
Thank you notes through the mail	Choice time
Having hot lunch at school	Music, stereo time/tapes, CDs
Books/reading a story	Pets/pet supplies
Posters	Special trips
Science kits	Dances/parties/evening events
Working on models/building kits	Telephone time/own phone
Gardening	Skateboarding
Playing games/board games/puzzles	Sporting event or concert
Magic tricks	Trip to arcade or laser tag venue

Some parents provide their children with a menu of incentives. Each incentive costs a certain number of points. Renting a movie might cost ten points. Making popcorn costs ten points. Having a friend over costs 15 points. This technique teaches children to save and budget their points. It also teaches them that good behavior and hard work are worth responsibility and freedom. Maintain high interest and motivation by changing the incentives. Every few weeks, add new items to the menu.

We find children are quite eager to work hard and behave well if they get something they like in return.

Phelecia: *We help our children understand that when they choose the right, and do the right thing, they get really good things. When they don't, then there are consequences. Perhaps they do not get a specific thing or privilege that they really wanted. I think that is much more effective than spanking, definitely, because it doesn't promote all those angry feelings. For discipline in the long-term, I think charts, contracts, and incentives are much more effective.*

"In the Moment" Discipline Strategies

Parent-child contracts and charts help parents teach children self-discipline over a long period of time. But there are times when we need to redirect behavior immediately, and for this we use our own version of the "time out" discipline strategy.

A "time out" is a way of setting limits. Setting limits can prevent misbehavior.

Phelecia: *I call our "time out" place the "happy chair." I think it's wonderful to be positive about taking time to think about behavior. We use it when our children have made poor choices. Perhaps our youngest child has hit one of the older children; perhaps our oldest daughter has refused to complete her homework; or maybe our middle child was rude. To change behavior "in the moment," we say, "You get to sit in the happy chair for five minutes."*

We are careful about how long children sit and think. "A minute for each year" is what we go by. So the four-year-old sits for four minutes, the six-year-old for six minutes, and so on. Sitting for, let's say, a half hour, seems too much. Children also need to understand that what they did wasn't right. When the time is up, we always ask, "What would you do differently?" We talk about that, so that the next time, the child will stop and think about his or her actions.

Brent: *When one of our kids makes a bad choice, he or she spends a few minutes in the "happy chair" or his or her bedroom. I let the child think about their choices for a while, and then I go in and give the child a hug. I say, "I love you." I also say that if I didn't love my children I would let them do whatever they wanted. But I love my children, so I set limits.*

Discipline In a Nutshell

We try to prevent our children from misbehaving by creating routines that teach self-discipline. When we have to discipline our children, we try to keep it as positive as possible by focusing on the behavior and not the child's character. We also notice and reward good behavior. Finally, we use discipline purposefully, and the purpose is not to control our children but to encourage cooperation.

We understand the real world of disciplining kids. Sometimes when your child misbehaves, you'll ask yourself: "What can I do so that my child learns from this experience, and so that he or she chooses not to do this again?" Other times, you will simply walk over and take the rubber snake away.

In the next chapter, we discuss the value of teaching values. We recommend instilling values "as old as the hills." We believe these values will also protect children from the real world by helping them to deal with the real world.

Chapter 6

"Would I Want You to Do That to Me?": Teaching G-Rated Values in an X-Rated World

Brent: *I remember one time coming home from a vacation in the mountains. We were in a hurry to get home like everybody else. Well, we hit traffic and all the cars started to slow down. The cars were bumper to bumper and people were honking.*

As I looked ahead, I realized that there was a man by himself, and his car had broken down. People were just belligerent; they were angry, you know, that this guy's car broke down and delayed them. It was only a two-lane road, one lane in each direction, so no one could get by.

Without even thinking, I got out. I pushed his car to the side and drove away and didn't think much of it.

The Golden Rule

Your kids watch you. As you do things each day, you teach them either G-Rated values or you teach them X-Rated values. It depends on how you parent. When we make choices we put our values into action. We can help children and teenagers make good choices by modeling good values.

VALUES IDEA BOX
The #1 Hatch Rule
In our home, the Golden Rule is number one; we remind our kids constantly: "Do unto others as you would have them do unto you."

Phelecia and I start with what Christians call the Golden Rule, but it is a value that is fundamental to many cultures and religions, and it says basically, "Do to others as you would have them do to you." The Golden Rule is also called the ethic of reciprocity, and it is found in the writings of nearly every religion, and some regard it as the most concise and general principle of ethics.

How universal is the Golden Rule? We found versions of it from 13 different spiritual traditions. While all are similar, taken together there is an even deeper wisdom as we recognize what a basic value the Golden Rule is. Children can understand that people worldwide acknowledge the importance of the Golden Rule, and that it should be applied to all people.

VALUES IDEA BOX		
The Golden Rule Across Three Religions		
Buddhism Treat not others in ways that you yourself would find hurtful. *The Buddha*, Udana-Varga 5.1	***Baha'i Faith*** Lay not on any soul a load that you would not wish to be laid upon you, and desire not for anyone the things you would not desire for yourself. *Baha'u'llah*, Gleanings	***Islam*** Not one of you truly believes until you wish for others what you wish for yourself. *The Prophet Muhammad*, 13th of the 40 Hadiths of Nawawi

Modeling Values

Phelecia: *I had an experience at our local elementary school. One woman who worked in the office was very angry, rude, curt, and generally offensive to everyone.*

I decided to take her on as a personal challenge. Our kids would say, "When she is in the office, she is so mean. She says, 'Stand over there until I get to you. What do you need?'" And my kids would say, "She doesn't even say, 'please.' It is so mean."

I explained that she must be hurting inside. Many people act like that when, really, what is wrong is that they are terribly unhappy with who they are. There might be things in their lives that are just sort of sad, so they can't be happy with other people.

So every week, once a week, I made cookies, and I would drop them off at the office. I remember the first time I dropped them off, she just kind of said, "Thank you," not in a real, you know, excited way.

And I thought, "Okay, that's all right. You know, I'm just going to kill her with kindness. I'm going to keep this up." The next week, I did the same thing, and she was actually in a nice mood.

For a year and a half, I took time to say hello, smile, and make sure I waved to her and just gave her the kindness that she deserved, that any human being deserves. At the end of a year and a half, she was my best friend. She was so kind and so sweet to me, and not just to me, but to others also, and to my kids as well.

What a transformation!

When you are met with an angry comment from somebody, it doesn't mean you should give an angry comment back. It is human nature, however, to hurt someone who has hurt you. But if you can try to remember the values of kindness and love for our fellow man, it would just make the world a better place, because love wins over anger and hate.

My experience with the offensive woman in the office was a good lesson for my children and me. My children saw adults working out relationships and becoming kinder. Now in their dealings with different people, they say things like, "Okay, mom, I know. I need to kill with kindness." When their friends are mean to them, I say, "You know, if you smile at someone long enough, even if they are frowning at you, eventually, they will smile back, because love does win."

Phelecia: *I try a little act of kindness at the grocery store. Before getting a cart for myself, I give a cart to the person behind me. It is interesting how surprised people are. My kids notice I do this. One time Ashlyne said, "That was nice, Mom, that you thought of somebody else first. I bet that made them feel really good." And I said, "I believe it does, it really does."*

I think that the compassion that you show to your children loving them, hugging them, and telling them what beautiful people they are, teaches them to go out in the world and do the same thing.

Teaching G-Rated Values Step by Step

Phelecia: *How can we present values to our children? I think that we teach best by our example, for children parrot what we do.*

For example, we had a homeless lady living on our block. One evening, she walked by and my children saw her. The four older children remarked, "She looks hungry, Mom. She doesn't look like she has any food." They were real concerned, and they wanted to give her some food.

We got some bread, peanut butter, and water, and when she came down the street again, I offered it to her. She said, "Thank you." The kids felt so good that they had done that, and they said, "Okay, good. She is not going to be hungry." Then in the morning, we found some of the food we had given her on our front porch with a note on it. She wrote, "I think you guys might need it more than me." I thought it was really sweet, because she knew how many kids we had. I think that was a neat thing that kindness begot kindness.

Parents can model values *and* help children to put this behavior into practice. This story is a good example and helps us understand that these situations have unexpected results.

Although we model values daily, our family also benefits from a step-by-step approach to teaching virtues and values. The suggestions that follow can help your children learn and practice values you believe are important. We suggest focusing on one value a month.

Once a year: Choose 12 Core Values

- Analyze the needs of your family and choose 12 core values to study over the coming year. For each month of the year, assign a value your family will study.

The chart below shows some of the values we have identified as important to our family. Take time to explore the values identified by your spiritual tradition or your own personal heroes or heroines. Identify for yourself and for your family the values you determine are important.

G-Rated Values			
Fairness	Caring	Citizenship	Courage
Generosity	Unselfishness	Justice	Politeness
Humor	Loyalty	Gratitude	Fidelity
Love	Respect	Humility	Self-Reliance
Tolerance	Honesty	Trustworthiness	Responsibility

Once a month: Discuss the Value's Meaning

- At the first Family Night of the month, discuss and analyze the month's value by answering the following who, what, where, why, and when questions:

To whom does this value apply? *or* Who demonstrates this value?
What is the meaning of this value?
Where can we show or see this value?
Why is this value important?
When do we use this value?

- Choose a story that illustrates the value or its opposite. In our family, we sometimes tell a story from the Bible or from our own experiences, such as the following story:

Brent: *We tell our children, "Sometimes doing the right thing isn't always the easiest thing." It is mostly the hard thing, but in the long run, it is the easier thing, since you feel better about it.*

I remember one time our middle daughter came home from school and said, "Well, I got my test back, and I got an 'A,' but then when I was looking it over, I noticed that the teacher made two mistakes which would have brought me down to a 'B.' I wanted an 'A,' but I marched right up to the teacher, and I told him the truth."

Folktales, fairy tales, and children's literature in general are a good source of stories to illustrate all sorts of values. See page 208 for suggestions.

Once a week: Give Rewards and Reinforce the Value

- At Family Night, talk about whether anyone demonstrated or witnessed someone else demonstrating the particular value. Ask, "Who is in the running for the [name of value] award?" Give out a paper award or a special privilege to a deserving member of the family.

- Games can help children and teens understand and implement values. By playing any board game children learn to take turns and practice good sportsmanship. Create your own games as well, such as, "Agree or Disagree." Write a list of simple scenarios on a large piece of paper, white board, or chalkboard. These scenarios should describe instances when a person did or did not show the particular value you are focusing on. As you read each scenario aloud, have your children raise their hands if they agree that the person is showing the value; let each child share his or her opinions and feelings.

Every day: Model and Praise

- Each day, model values for your children and take time to praise any efforts they make towards implementing these values themselves. Try to ignore times when they make a misstep (unless it is serious and warrants action) and praise their positive behavior and efforts.

Phelecia: *When one of our sons was in first grade, he came home from school and showed me a trading card a friend had "given" to him. Parents of young boys learn quickly about the latest trading-card craze. We also know that boys don't just give away their best cards. Since our son had no cards to trade, I suspected that something was not right.*

A little while later, he confessed to me that he had actually taken this card from his friend.

"Would you want someone to steal from you?" I asked.

"No. But my friend just left it in his backpack," he explained.

"Of course he did! That's where he was keeping it for safety. You need to return the card and apologize," I said gently.

Our son didn't want to do this, because he knew his friend would be mad and he didn't want his friend to hate him. I explained that part of taking something is returning it. He asked if I would come with him to return it, so I did. The little boy was so delighted to have the card back that he didn't really even care that our son had taken it.

Sometimes, we are embarrassed when our children do things like that, and we think it would be easier just to forget the whole thing. I think it's important to make sure that when a wrong has been done we help them make it right. This makes children think about their actions for next time.

To help your child put values into action, consider adding to his or her daily chores an activity that reinforces a value. For example, if you want your child to be unselfish or sensitive to others add, "Do a good deed" to the child's chore chart. One parent reported to us that when her seven-year-old son saw, "Do a good deed" on his chart, he asked, "What's a good deed?" This mother smiled to herself and thought, "That is exactly why he needs this item on his chart."

Including activities that reinforce values in a child's daily chores will make the values real for the child and, possibly will open up a discussion of how to be honest, courageous, or respectful, etc.

Making Choices

Values Idea Box	
Values in Action	
Value	***Action***
Honesty	If someone says or does something that is mean, be truthful about how it made you feel instead of getting angry with them in return.
Courage	Say hello to a classmate at your school to whom you don't usually talk.
Self-Reliance, Potential	Think of something that is difficult for you to do and find a way to make it easier (e.g. Take the activity and break it down into smaller, easier-to-do tasks.).
Discipline, Moderation	Try not to eat any sweets for three days.
Respect	Open a door for someone else and let that person go before you.
Love	Give a hug to a family member or pet.
Unselfishness, Sensitivity	Do a good deed.
Kindness, Friendliness	Help a friend with something.

Brent: *I believe that children with good values can be pretty lonely. Not in a bad way, but you have got to stand your ground, and sometimes that means doing things that no one else is doing.*

When I was a kid we lived on a farm, and I would walk to the bus stop about a mile away. I was constantly asked if I wanted drugs. Older kids put stuff in front of me. "Do you want to do drugs? Do you want to do this? Do you want to do that?"

Luckily, I had parents who raised me right. They taught me good moral values. I knew what my answer was going to be, and after a while, these people wouldn't ask me anymore.

But refusing offers for drugs, cigarettes, and sex also meant that I was left out of certain social groups, activities, and even parties. I felt a little lonely, but I also didn't want to do a lot of the things they were doing.

Children *can* learn to make sound choices based on our universally accepted values, if we allow them to make less profound choices when they are young, such as, "Do you want juice in the red cup or the blue?" or "Which sweater will you wear today?" These choices may seem insignificant to adults but the process of choosing helps the child feel competent.

Sue Spayth Riley explains the importance of choices in her book, *How to Generate Values in Young Children*. "As a parent and teacher I am fascinated by the importance of developing the decision-making capabilities of young children. These capabilities are their foundation for the growth of reason, judgment, creativity, and—of the utmost importance—their self-esteem and ability to formulate values."[31]

Parents must remain the authority in areas involving safety, bed time, meal time, and general health. However, once we have created a safe environment, children should be allowed to make choices concerning toys, art projects, and general play.

Here are some tips for maintaining control and order in your home while allowing your child to make choices:

- Analyze and understand your child's temperament and decide how much choice he or she can handle. Some children are willful and thrive on choice. Others find choices overwhelming and confusing.
- Choose areas for complete parental authority: safety issues (seat belt, car seat, bike helmet, sunscreen, etc.); meal times; bed times; daily routine; TV viewing, etc.
- Consider those areas that are open to negotiation. For instance, the child or teen must complete his or her homework after school, but he or she can decide to relax first, then complete assignments. The parent chooses the bed time, but the child can choose to read for a while before going to sleep. The child or teen must eat dinner, but if he or she does not like the meal being served, a food that requires no extra preparation from the parent can be substituted. The child must brush his or her teeth, but can choose his or her favorite type of toothbrush, toothpaste, and floss.

Make Choices, Learn Values

Phelecia: *When one of our sons was 11, he took a singing class. Before the first class, I told him about a boy his age, Kyle, who would be in the class. Kyle was born with several physical disabilities. Anyway, I told my son about Kyle and my son said, "Oh, I will stand by him, Mom. I will help him, whatever he needs."*

So our son did that, and they had a wonderful time. After class, our son said that he couldn't understand why other people wouldn't want to be with Kyle. He said they wouldn't help him, and that they weren't being very kind to him. I remember our son saying, "Why, mom? He's such a beautiful person."

Thank goodness my son has compassion and love for other people; he wants to help other people. And, to me, this is such a beautiful attitude, because the most difficult thing is to accept other people who are different. You need to love yourself enough to be able to love those around you.

This story illustrates the kind of choices we want all children to make. Our son was kind and generous while his peers were not. We believe he was able to demonstrate solid values because he has seen them modeled so frequently at home.

Brent: *We had just gotten home from watching Fourth of July fireworks, when our then eight-year-old daughter told me that there had been a man walking in front of her and she saw money had fallen out of his pocket. She quickly ran to catch up to him to return the money. It was about $40 and the guy was very happy and thankful. Phelecia and I were pleased, because our daughter didn't think twice about the right thing to do. She saw the money, knew it wasn't hers, and returned it. She wanted to do the right thing.*

Children can deal with the real world if they are given the right tools. Instilling sound values is as important as protecting children. Values can help children cope with the real world, but what else can we do? In the next chapter we discuss the importance of building self-esteem by loving children unconditionally.

Chapter 7

"I Will Always Love You...": Nurture Your Family with Unconditional Love

Phelecia: *One day, I found out that our son had told a lie. When I asked him about it, he said, "I was afraid to tell you, Mom, I thought maybe you wouldn't love me anymore." I said, "Son, I will always love you. I might not like a choice you have made, but, no matter what, I will always love you."*

Children need to understand that no matter what they do or how they act, their parents will always love them and accept them. Our children are worthy of love, and so we love them. This is the definition of unconditional love.

Each day we have so many opportunities to show our children unconditional love. The minute they wake up, we can greet them with warm words and loving arms. Providing a structure to the day lets children know we care so much about them, we have taken the time to have healthy meals, clean clothes, and a safe, secure environment.

Show your children that you love them enough to keep them safe and out of harm's way. Instead of yelling at them to follow safety rules, say, "I care for you so much, I can't let you ride your bike without a helmet." "You are important to me, so I want you to stay out of the street when you ride your scooter." "What you are doing doesn't look safe and makes me worry."

When your child struggles with difficult schoolwork, problems with friends, or any challenge, remind your child of your faith in him or her to solve problems. Give them words of encouragement: "I believe in you." "I know you can do it." "We're good thinkers; let's find a way to solve this problem."

You love your child, and your job is to let him or her know it. Find out what makes them feel loved. Do lots of loving hugs do the trick? Does your child want to spent time reading a story one on one or playing a game of catch? Perhaps having a delicious, healthy snack waiting for him or her after school says to your child, "Mom/Dad really loves me." So often parents at our seminars say, "But, of course, I love my child; he/she must know that." Make certain your children know you love them. If your children are very young, simply observe what makes them calm, relaxed, and happy. You can ask an older child, "What makes you feel really loved and cared for?" Then all you need to do is follow through.

Unconditional Love on TV

As you model unconditional love, be mindful of the negative messages about love and family in the media today. On the whole, the media focuses on dysfunctional families because of the need for drama and excitement. Fortunately, you are your child's first teacher, and you can teach him or her to be critical of the media.

Ask your children to think about the families they see on TV. Does TV depict real families? Discuss whether TV families solve problems the way real families do, or if they even talk like real families. You can counteract negative effects of the media by showing and telling your children about normal, real families. You can also carefully select which media products your children are exposed to. (For more tips on screening all type of media, see Appendix 1.)

Elements of Unconditional Love: Time, Praise, Empathy, and Respect

Brent: *I hear it all the time: "I work constantly! I'm always gone. I have got to work, work, and work." This is not good. If your life is that busy, then you need to stop, step back, and think, what is really important?*

On your deathbed you are not going to lie there thinking, "Boy, I wish I had spent more time at the office." You are going to wish you spent more time with your spouse, your kids, and your family. That is what it is all about. You can't take money with you, but when you are gone, your kids are going to have memories of the time you spent with them.

There are many, many parts or elements of unconditional love, but we've identified things that we feel are important. A child feels loved when he or she gets your time, praise, empathy, and respect. Let's start with time.

Time

A child needs the undivided attention of his or her parent or caregiver for a little while each day. We have a large household, but we make sure each child gets that. We also make sure each child gets special time alone with Brent each week, since the kids spend most of their time each day with Phelecia. The "special" child gets to pick out where he or she wants to go, and we make sure everybody gets a turn. It is really a pleasant time for Brent and the kids, and it strengthens the parent-child bond. Sometimes children are ready to share their thoughts and feelings during scheduled quality time, but we have found that they also open up and talk during mundane day-to-day tasks. Any kind of time that you spend really listening to your child is great.

Praise

Brent: *In watching other families, I have noticed a lot of parents who are just constantly angry with their kids. It seems like they are always mad!*

Make a conscious effort every day to praise and compliment your child. Constant criticism and nagging does not bring a happy spirit. It does not make children feel good about themselves or about your love for them. We believe they can even begin to feel you don't love them or appreciate them. Then you end up with hostile, negative kids who are unwilling to share their feelings with you.

Children can get many negative messages during the day. They get these messages at school for not being the smartest, best dressed, or most talented athlete; or from the media, which tries to make us all feel inadequate if we do not have the latest gizmo or toy. We can make our homes a place where children hear positive messages by complimenting our children every day. The following comments are so easy to say and yet have a powerful impact on self-esteem: "Thanks so much for doing your chores." "You are such a handsome boy." "You are such a strong, smart, beautiful girl."

Brent: *I was eating breakfast with the kids, and I happened to be dressed up for a client meeting. Suddenly, one of the kids hit a tall glass of milk with an elbow and I was covered in milk. It splashed on three of the kids as well, and we had five minute to get out the door. I wanted to scream.*

Over the years, Phelecia and I have learned not to yell over spilled milk (or other minor, yet major, disasters), but it hasn't been easy. What we have learned from raising seven children is that you need perspective. If a mistake is made, make that an opportunity to learn and grow; it is not the end of the world. Focus instead on fixing the mistake together, without shame or blame. Parents can create memories for their children, and we want them to be wonderful memories of love and caring. That is our goal.

Phelecia: *We need to relish our children. There are days when you will feel like giving up, but you must look at the broader picture; the end of the rainbow, as it were. Parents often think, "Why is this happening to me?" or "Why do I have to deal with this now?" I like to say to myself, "What can I learn from this?" I think it is important to appreciate your role as parents. We all need to figure out ways to deal with the difficulties of parenting and find strategies that bring us closer to our children. We are so blessed to have the chance to be parents; it is an opportunity that is so rewarding and special.*

Empathy and Respect

Two other building blocks of unconditional love are empathy and respect. We show our children we empathize with them and respect them when we validate their feelings. This makes most people feel understood, loved, and respected. Everybody must be validated, but especially children. You can even validate your child's feelings when you ask him or her to do something. Here are some examples:

Instead of this:	***Try talking to your child respectfully:***
"Go do your jobs. Do them now and do a better job than you did before."	"Hey, James, I really like the way you did the dishes last night. Tonight, could you do just as good a job? That really helped us out. You did an awesome job."
"Kids, get in the car. And no whining about leaving the park. We're going NOW!"	"We need to leave the park in five minutes. I know you've had fun and that it's hard to leave. What is the last thing you want to do before we go?"
"Stop fighting over that dumb toy! You two are old enough to share. Stop being babies about it and take turns."	"I see that you and Jason are having trouble sharing the water balloon slingshot. Can you two find a way to share it, or should you choose a different game?"

Brent: *If no one validates your feelings, then you feel like no one cares and I think this creates feelings of low self-esteem. Everybody wants to be validated—both children and adults.*

Another way to validate your child's point of view is by noticing his or her feelings before he or she says a word.

Phelecia: *I try to "read" my kids' moods. When I can tell one of them is upset or down, I ask what he or she needs and how we can work together to help.*

My son was watching TV recently and I noticed he was cold. I went and got a blanket and put it in the dryer so it was nice and warm, and then I laid it on him. He said, "Thank you, Mom. That was really nice of you." A few days later, he did the same thing for me when he noticed I was cold.

When one of my daughters is having a hard time with her hair, I'll just jump in and help her. When she sees that the two-year-old is having a hard time with something, she'll go over and help him with it.

At the end of a long day, my eldest son will sometimes say, "Mom, you sit down and let me rub your feet for you."

Love really does beget love! Respect begets respect.

It is also crucial to show empathy by validating feelings when something has happened to your child—whether it is real or perceived. We try to keep our own opinions of what has happened to ourselves, and instead say such things as, "I'm sorry you are so sad today," or, "I'm sorry if I hurt your feelings." The key is to validate and not dismiss your children's feelings. We believe this strategy helps children and others feel unconditionally loved.

Brent: *I often think about unconditional love as a grand circle. If you give your kids unconditional love and respect, you get it back. And, hopefully, the circle will grow grander still as they seek out the same kind of love and respect in their marriages and relationships with their children.*

Setting Limits

Giving unconditional love does not mean that children should think, "Okay, my parents love me, no matter what. I can go out and do everything wrong, and they will just keep loving me." We will love them, but they need to know that choices have consequences, ultimately.

Set limits and have rules, but let your children have a say. Of course, you will decide on safety rules, bed times, and meal times, but where they can give input, let them. Use family meetings to discuss limits and problems that your family might be having. This strategy models the values of cooperation and fairness.

When children do misbehave or break a rule, let the consequence be natural and let them have second chances. If a child spills milk, he or she needs to help clean it up. If your child spills again, consider getting a cup with a lid!

Unconditional Love Idea Box

What Can Parents Do and What Can They Avoid to Show Unconditional Love?

Avoid the following:	***Do the following instead:***
Ruling your children like a dictator	Set simple, fair rules with natural consequences for misbehavior
Yelling and nagging	Listen and speak respectfully to your child
Rushing and working constantly	Spend time with your children
Criticism and negative comments	Give praise and compliments
Dismissing or minimizing their feelings or thoughts	Empathize with their feelings
Belittling their feelings, thoughts, and ideas	Respect their feelings

Don't Forget the Hugs!

Brent: About 15 years ago, my brother and I came up a product called The Hug Card. It's a plastic card the size and shape of a credit card and it has a small heat-sensitive square on it. To use the card, you place your thumb on the heat-sensitive square. After ten seconds, the square turns a different color. If it's black, you need four hugs; if it's blue you need three hugs; and so on. My brother and I thought it was a neat interactive tool; an "ice breaker." We thought we would sell a few to card stores. We have now sold more than three-and-a-half million Hug Cards all over the world. We receive letters all the time from folks telling us what a powerful instrument it is to help people reach out and connect to others in a positive way.

Hugging is one of the most important gifts we can give our children. When parents hug each other or their kids, it brings a sense of peace and security to the home. Hugging makes one feel loved and cared for. We believe there is something about hugging that can heal. When a baby is born, he or she is placed right in Mom's arms, for we understand that babies thrive when they are held. Part of the treatment for premature infants is to hold them for a period of time each day right on the parent's skin. Hugging seems to help those who suffer from everything from depression to anorexia.

Yet, some parents are afraid that hugging their kids will make them weak. The opposite is true; it will make your child stronger. If you haven't hugged your kids much, he or she might resist, but just keep hugging! In one of our seminars, a mom told us that her teenager brought home The Hug Card and it transformed their relationship. The mom had stopped hugging the child as she grew older but the child, now a teen, still wanted hugs but didn't know how to ask. So make hugging part of your routine, even if your children are young adults.

Adults themselves need hugs. At one seminar, I went over to a woman and gave her a big hug. She later told me she had never been hugged! We gave out about 50 Hug Cards at another seminar and transformed a room of 50 serious adults into a group of hugging, laughing people. The Hug Card simply gives us all permission to give and get the love we need.

Create a Loving Home

If you want your child to make good choices, then love them unconditionally. Children who feel loved have higher self-esteem. Children with high self-esteem feel empowered to make constructive, rather than destructive, choices. They make G-Rated choices!

Here are ten easy ways to show your children unconditional love today:

1. Hug your children.
2. Praise and compliment them.
3. Do not yell or nag.
4. Spend time with your children.
5. Listen to your children.
6. Respect their feelings.
7. Set limits.
8. Encourage them.
9. Focus on the positive.
10. Treat mistakes as opportunities; do not belittle or shame.

A quick hug, a loving word, and a listening ear are all simple actions that will make your child feel loved. Some of us, however, find these simple actions quite difficult because of childhood experiences. In the next chapter, we will offer ideas that can help you overcome emotional challenges, so that you will be free to unconditionally love your children, your spouse, and yourself.

Chapter 8

"...But First I Need to Love Myself": Nurture Yourself with Unconditional Love

When people marry, they vow to stay together "for richer or poorer." Most couples probably assume that they will only struggle with not being as rich as they had wished. We lived through a time of being very poor, and our unconditional love for each other was tested.

Brent: *I haven't talked about this rough patch in my life too much, because it was a painful time for me. It happened in the mid-1990s during an extremely rainy fall and winter in California. Rain has a huge effect on my car-detailing business, because I mostly work outside. Yet the rain was only one of the challenges we faced that winter. The engine on my truck blew, and the mechanics replaced it with the wrong engine. The back of our house completely flooded every time it rained. We were completely broke, and then our sixth child was born.*

Frankly, I felt like crap, because I could not provide for my family.

Phelecia: *One afternoon Brent couldn't find something, and the frustrations of months and months of rain, mishaps, and hardship finally got to him. He pulled all the drawers out of the dressers and threw everything out on the floor. His rage increased until he was out of control, so the kids and I left.*

After a few hours, I called home and got no answer. I didn't want the kids to see how worried I was, so I asked a friend to watch them for a bit. I drove home.

Our house was straightened up, but Brent was gone. His phone and pager, which never left his side, were there. Panic overtook me; my legs felt weak and my heart raced. Should I have left him alone? Was he suicidal? Where was he?

I think we have all felt worthless at times, and such feelings can instantly make us depressed. We look around and see how great everyone else's lives are. But everyone is looking at everyone else. It is important for us to know how much worth we have. That feeling of worthlessness needs to be fought. Think about all your good qualities and the positive things you have. Let others know how much you need them—especially your spouse or partner and child. All a child wants is love and acceptance, not material things.

Phelecia: *I went back to my friend's house, got the children, and went home. The kids wanted to know what happened to their dad. I told them that he needed time to be alone and he would be back soon. Inside I was absolutely dying, because I didn't know what was going to happen. I told myself to have faith that he would be all right.*

I realized Brent might not have enough money to call home, so I activated our toll-free business number. The phone rang and I answered it, but no one responded. Just as the other end of line went dead, it hit me that it was Brent. The phone rang once more, and again there was silence. I started talking to the emptiness and said how much I loved him.

Brent started talking, and he sounded upset and depressed. He told me that the kids and I deserved better, someone who could provide for us.

I told him I would come get him. He said he was going away because he couldn't provide for us. He had hit bottom and felt like he wasn't worth anything to me. I reassured him how much the kids and I loved him and cared about him.

Phelecia: *I was so happy that I was able to speak to Brent in a loving manner instead of being angry that he had left without telling me where he was going. I was happy that I knew instantly to speak sweetly and let him know that it was safe to come back home.*

How did the story with Brent end? We called some of his really good friends and they brought him home. The rain finally stopped.

In the film, *It's A Wonderful Life*, Jimmy Stewart's character has everything of real value, such as love and respect. Yet at one point in his life, he feels worthless. We all can relate to those feelings, but we can also all rise above these feelings.

Break the Chain of Negativity

Brent: *I've found that people just don't love themselves. But to invite love into your home, you need love in your heart.*

Loving yourself first is critical, because if you don't love yourself, you can't love other people. Find the good and even the less good parts of yourself and embrace them; then you can teach your children about love. We have to love ourselves first before we can show our kids love. Yet as the following story from a friend illustrates, that can be a challenge for those who were rejected by their parents.

I was the youngest of nine children and was raised by parents steeped in the ancient Chinese religions and superstitions of their ancestors. All of my siblings had to drop out of school after they finished junior high school and start working to help support the family.

I, on the other hand, had different plans. From the time I was young, I had no intention of working on a farm like my parents or working in a factory like my older brothers or sisters. When I was 14 years old, my parents told me it was time to leave school and go to work. I told them that I would not and that I was going to continue on with my schooling in the fall. They were shocked. Where had I gotten the nerve to disobey them? I had always been an obedient, well-behaved child.

My parents did not think women should be educated. They said I could live at home only if I helped support the family, and if I didn't, I would have to leave home and never come back. As hard as it was, even in the face of ever-increasing verbal and physical abuse, at age 14, I left home.

I got a job in a factory, assembling simple electronic components, much the same fate that I left home in order to avoid. But, I was free to pursue what I felt was important. I lived in the company dormitory and attended school when I wasn't working.

I had thought that if I paid my own way in life that my parents would be happy and forgive me for leaving home. This was not the case. They were angry with me because my money was going toward my education and not to them. Each time I returned home to visit, they refused to speak with me. I don't know why I kept going back. Each time, I went home with hope and left with tears.

Over the next three years, the situation grew worse. Their resentment and anger towards me grew to the point that they told me they no longer considered me their daughter, telling me so directly to my face and in front of family, friends, and neighbors. Occasionally, there were even threats of violence from my father, but this was mainly the effect of his alcohol abuse, and he never actually hurt me physically.

Many times I wondered if I had made the right choice. I was disappointed in my family, and I was confused about the purpose of life. The feeling I got from my parents was that money was more important than family.

Years passed and I continued my education and made wonderful friends who became my new, supportive family. No one from my family attended my wedding. My marriage brought the now familiar response from my parents. I cried and felt disappointed when they told me to "never come home again." But this time I did not feel like an orphan, because I had started my own family, the family I always wanted.

As this story illustrates, life is hard for those of us who have had challenging childhoods. But nearly everyone has wounds from childhood. These wounds can be severe or minor, but they all affect how we parent. The good news is that you can change. You can break the chains of negativity in your life, if you are willing to look at what hurt you and how it made you feel. This can be difficult and emotional, but the bonus is this: when you keep your own children from getting hurt in the same ways, you heal yourself.

Nurturing Idea Box

We have to find out what makes us happy, loved, and feel good about ourselves. An old saying reminds us that people wrapped up in themselves make pretty small packages. We agree and believe that service helps one find love. When you serve other people, when you fulfill the needs of others, you find love. All you have to do is lose yourself in service to others. You will teach yourself about love and teach your children how to love.

Start healing yourself the next time your child pushes your buttons. Psychologists will tell you that when your child does something to push your buttons, that something probably gave you trouble as a child.

Brent: *I came home one evening and the house was a mess: the laundry wasn't done, the kids were running around, and dinner wasn't ready. I got mad and yelled. I said terrible things to the kids and Phelecia.*

Phelecia calmly asked me to leave and suggested I come back when I was calm.

I sat in a park by myself thinking about what an idiot I was. I was a jerk to the people I love the most!

After this incident, Phelecia and I talked, which really helped, but I also put a "no yelling" reminder on the wall. During our next family meeting, we let each child share feelings about yelling and anger. We listened without judgment, and tried to summarize their thoughts. I talked about my own issues, and I also made a request. I asked the kids to get their chores done earlier for the next two weeks, and told them if they did so, we'd have a treat. Then I did a great imitation of myself getting really mad; the kids started mimicking me, and we all had a great laugh.

Brent: *I think it's good to sit down with your spouse, a friend, or even just yourself, and think what you can do to improve yourself. Work on one thing at a time. I think that's what we've done. I've got to work on my temper. My daughter reminds me, "Dad, don't raise your voice. The only time you should raise your voice is in case of a fire." Our kids should see that we are trying to work on things. That's what we've done, and I'm better than I was ten years ago.*

Unconditional love starts when good behavior ends! When your kids push your buttons, try exploring your own issues, and you will become a better parent. Combine this with some good communication skills, and you've got a powerful boost to your parenting. (For more on communication skills, see Chapter 4).

Protect Yourself

The psychologist and author, Dr. Sal Severe, suggests protecting yourself against what he calls button-pushing attacks. "Some parents," he says, "find it helpful to have a technique that diffuses their anger. Go sit in your room for a few minutes. Listen to music. Go for a walk. Count to 25. Think peaceful thoughts. Reward yourself when you do survive a button attack."

Dr. Severe also encourages parents to make a plan to change their reactions. We've added an extra step—think about the event to understand it better. Here's an example of a situation that can trigger upset, as well as a plan to change the reaction.

Button Pusher: Your children argue.

"In the Moment" Plan:

I will stay calm—I won't get angry or yell.

If I get angry, I will go sit in my room.

I will cool off before I say anything.

I will let it out slowly.

I won't save anger until it erupts.

I will say: "I feel angry when you argue like that."

I will spotlight the positive; focus on cooperation.

I will look for times when my children agree.

"In a Quiet Moment" Plan:

I will think about how my parents reacted when my siblings and I argued. I'll find a specific example that gave me joy or pain.

I will explore my feelings about this issue.

I will talk about it with my partner or a friend.

I will use this new understanding to help me deal with the same situation in the future.

These things "push my buttons":	***Here's how my own parents reacted to this situation when I was a child:***	***I now understand that I react this way because:***	***My plan to change my reaction to the situation in the future includes:***
Brent: Kids "forget" chores; house and yard a mess.	*"They got mad, told us we were bad, and told us to clean up."*	*"My parents didn't take time to discuss the problem; they just yelled."*	*Stay calm! Talk to Phelecia about my issues. Call family meeting. Present options for fixing problem and offer reward.*
Phelecia: Older children wanting to date and be independent.	*"Sometimes we had lots of supervision, but at other times we were on our own."*	*"I want to find the right balance between protecting my children and trusting that they will make good decisions."*	*Stay calm. Talk to Brent about my feelings. Step back and trust that our children will uphold our standards and follow our rules.*
The space below is for you to use:			

Make a list of behaviors that push your buttons. Think about the possible causes, and then write out a plan to deal with each. Phelecia and I have each listed our favorite "button pushers" and strategies to change our reactions. We have also left blank spaces for you to use to work on your own issues.

By confronting the situations that bother you the most and making plans to change your reactions, you will reduce the amount of yelling and negativity in your day-to-day family life. You, your children, and your partner will feel more love and less negativity. We guarantee that you will all feel that love is unconditional in your household.

Take a Break from Parenting

Brent: *Phelecia and I have never stopped dating. We go out once a week, no matter what. Friends ask us, "How do you guys afford to go out to dinner all the time—it so expensive." But can you afford not to work on your primary relationship? As far as the expense goes, you are either going to pay for it now or pay for it later. Dinner and a movie cost a lot less than couple's therapy! We try not to forget that when the kids are grown up and living on their own, it will be the two of us alone once again.*

Your adult relationships will give you the strength to love your children unconditionally. It is not selfish to focus on nurturing yourself and relationships with friends, your spouse, partner, or family; it is essential. Think of it this way: if you were on an airplane with your kids and the oxygen masks dropped from the compartment above you, what would you do first? Would you grab your mask or the one for your child? *You would put your own mask on first, and then help your child.* You are not much help to your kids if you are turning blue and gasping for breath! The time you take to nurture yourself and your adult relationships is like oxygen, and it will give new life to your parenting.

Phelecia: *All couples have problems at times, but our relationship is about working through the tough times together, and our "date nights" really help. It's just great to share each other's company and to speak to each other without interruptions.*

Brent: *Even at times when we didn't have any money, Phelecia and I made sure we still went out. We'd buy a cheap dessert and sit and talk or just get out and spend time together.*

Always remember to date and court each other because it reminds you why you married, and that keeps your marriage alive. It's the little things that mean a lot. It's not about buying expensive gifts. It's the gifts of time and companionship that make you feel thankful that you are together.

Phelecia: *Date night helps to remind you of why you got married, plus you get the chance to enjoy each other's company. Sometimes Brent will bring me flowers or surprise me or sing a song for me. When I was away at a retreat, a huge bouquet of flowers was delivered to me. I remember thinking how thoughtful that was. Brent does that often, he'll bring me flowers for no reason, any occasion, just because he's thinking about me. If I'm having a hard time he'll take me out to dinner or take me on a walk. It's so important to remember why you married one another and keep that sparkle alive. When we dated, Brent worked for a limo company and did a lot of funeral drop-offs. Every Thursday the cemetery would take all the flowers and throw them in the trash, so Brent would go on that day and get a huge bouquet of flowers for our regular Friday-night date.*

Brent: *Phelecia didn't know the flowers had been thrown away—it's important to be creative about romance when money is tight. We have our own way of saying "I love you" when we're out in public and saying personal things is not appropriate. When we're holding hands, I'll squeeze Phelecia's hand three times and she knows that means "I love you." Little gestures like that are so important.*

Phelecia: *One of the things that attracted me to Brent is he's always so spontaneous and not afraid to do things in front of other people. He'll always leave me little notes or messages on my cell phone and I do the same for Brent. I know his favorite kind of candy and leave it for him.*

Brent: *Out of the blue, Phelecia will call me and tell me how much she appreciates what I do. Sometimes she puts a note in my lunch. Those little things are priceless and mean a lot.*

Dating is very important to keep that spirit and flame alive with your partner. With 50 to 60 percent of Americans getting divorced it's getting scary. Protect your marriage by doing the same things you did when you were courting or first married. We believe that one reason people divorce is because they forget to keep the spark of love alive. When we were going to be married, a woman told Phelecia that she could stop wearing make-up and dressing up. We both thought that was such a sad comment, because that is actually when you need to do those things the most.

Phelecia: *When we had been married about ten years, we took a trip to Big Bear; just the two of us.*

Brent wrote "Just Married" with shaving cream on the back of the car and even tied metal cans to the rear bumper! It was very cute to think about the day ten years before that we were married.

Getting away from the kids, enjoying each other's company, and remembering why we married made us both feel that our life together was properly balanced between meeting our children's needs and meeting our own.

Life gets crazy when you have kids! Sometimes you get upset with your partner, but it is always important to remind yourself that you are on the same team. Try to build a strong, healthy connection and support each other emotionally.

Phelecia: *Some times, we couldn't afford babysitters. So I would create a pretend date night for us. I would cook one of Brent's favorite dinners, then set a fancy table, light candles, and chill sparkling cider. When he arrived home, I would have a nice hot bath waiting for him and meet him at the door with his bathrobe. I would get the kids involved by having them act as waiters and waitresses for us.*

Single parents face an extra burden, and you should not expect yourself to "do it all" alone. Reach out to friends who can support you emotionally, or at least watch your children while you do something that renews your spirit.

Nurturing Idea Box

Check It Out: Parents' Night Out

Many YMCAs, preschools, and day-care centers offer a "Parents' Night Out." Usually the cost is reasonable (cheaper than a sitter), the kids have a great time, and parents get some time to themselves.

Phelecia: *Have you ever had one of those days when you feel like you're not doing anything right and everything is falling apart? It seems as though everything your children say to you is upsetting you because you're not happy with yourself, plus you're overwhelmed by the amount of responsibility you have—and everything seems multiplied by 50,000.*

When I've had those times, it's so nice to be able to have Brent come home and say, "Let's go out and have some alone time, take a break, talk to each other without any interruptions."

The time you spend away from your children makes you feel like a new person. Brent and I usually come home refreshed and ready to face any challenge.

Let your children see the love that you have for one another or for yourself. Children feel so secure when they see their parents hug or exchange nice words. When you take time for yourself by exercising, going out with friends, or doing anything fulfilling, you are acting as a good role model. Your children will learn to take time to nurture themselves too.

Brent: *Don't just bring flowers for birthdays and Valentine's Day, do it all the time—be spontaneous!*

Phelecia: *Our children see Brent bring me flowers, so he is a great role model for them.*

Phelecia: *I write little notes for Brent that say, "I want you to know how much I appreciate you;" "You do a lot of hard work for us, and I appreciate it."*

Brent: *Surprise your wife by doing the dishes or washing the clothes when she is gone. Forget "traditional" roles! We are all in this together.*

When parents help each other, they can overcome almost any challenge. One simple thing couples can do is to find time to nurture and love each other; single parents can do the same with the help of friends and family. Taking time to nurture yourself will give you the strength and resources to love your children more fully.

CHAPTER 9

"CHOOSE THE RIGHT": EMBRACE HAPPINESS EVERY DAY

Brent: *"We are as happy as we make our minds up to be," Abraham Lincoln is believed to have said. Happiness is not the state of your bank account, your career, your relationships, or even your health. Happiness is a state of mind, and you can choose to embrace happiness in spite of challenging circumstances.*

Perhaps your immediate circumstances make it hard for you to embrace happiness. Phelecia and I struggle with the ups and downs of my business income, and this creates its own tensions. Since we have a large family, there is usually a child going through a difficult time developmentally, and that can put extra stress on us as we struggle to find appropriate parenting strategies.

We understand how each day can bring challenges that range from the mundane (e.g. "How can we pay all these bills?") to the profound (e.g. "How can we raise good, happy children?"). But we cannot wait for happiness to find us when our income is higher and our children all "perfect." When we accept happiness as a state of mind, we are free to feel joy and bliss in spite of difficulties.

Phelecia: *Happiness means different things to everyone. We have found great happiness through our marriage, our children, and* *our religion. Others find fulfillment in intellectual pursuits, their careers, their friends.*

If you won millions of dollars tomorrow would you be happier than you are today? Psychologists have studied lottery winners and found that, although their lives change in material ways (better house, cars, vacations, etc.), after a period of time, these people report that they feel as happy after their windfall as they did before. And what if you lost something you considered a cornerstone of your happiness?

Phelecia: *A close friend was diagnosed with lymphoma last year, and we have witnessed the changes in her life. During her cancer treatment, friends helped her out by taking care of her daughters, cooking meals, and running errands. In the depths of her illness, once she had time to process her predicament, she reported that she was never happier. "I am so happy to be alive; I thought I had an appreciation for life, but now I savor each day and each experience—positive or negative. I cherish my life, however long or short it might be."*

Experts tell us that windfalls and disasters do not necessarily bring happiness or great sadness, and that your frame of mind can affect your happiness. However, no one has ever said that working to be happy was easy!

Brent: *What can unhappy families do to be happy? I think it starts at the top. Parents must be happy first. Yours is the first face that your kids will see each day. If you are happy and show them kindness, they will at least grow up in a happy atmosphere.*

It starts with you, and it's not easy. I feel such stress over my responsibilities as a parent. I have to make money, be a good husband and parent, and keep smiling. I am fortunate enough to have a wife who lifts me up when I am depressed. And when she is depressed, which is really rare, I try to help her and lift her up. I think as husband and wife we need to lift each other up whatever the issue. That's what we have done.

We know people who are very unhappy, but who have turned their lives around. It is a choice. Are you going to be happy in a situation? Are you going to look for the positive? You can choose to be really angry or to be happy about any given situation. If you are going through a rough patch, even then, try to find the positive things you can learn.

There are some people who need medical attention for chronic depression and unhappiness. As parents we need to watch for warning signs in our own children and seek help from a doctor when necessary. But in general, deciding to be happy and finding happiness with who you are is a choice that can lead to happiness.

Brent: *Parents who find their kids are depressed have to constantly motivate them. Kids get depressed about homework, dating, and what they are going to wear. You have to be positive and constantly tell them how good they are and how good they look. If you sense your child is down, and you don't know what is wrong, talk it out with him and help him figure out what good can come of the situation or his feelings.*

Although happiness is a state of mind, our choices also affect our happiness, and there are choices families can make that help lead to happiness.

Setting Goals Leads to Happiness

To help our children find happiness in their own lives, we encourage them to set goals and consider their priorities. Brent takes time with each child, and together they write out goals for different areas. They talk about ways to reach these goals, and they write the goal and the action plan on a chart. Then both Brent and the child commit to the goals with a signature.

Here's an example:

My Goals: McKay			
Area	***Goal***	***To Do***	***Signatures***
School	Raise math grade to B+.	Practice math skills each night	
Home	Control temper when younger kids are bothering me.	1. Talk to siblings about when I want to play and when I don't. 2. Tell brother/sister I need to leave the room when I am upset. 3. Ask Mom and Dad for help.	
Friends	Be loyal.	If friends start to gossip or cut down others, I will not participate. I will change the subject or walk away.	
Community	Help those less fortunate.	Give some of my allowance to a good cause.	
Personal	Take a 50-mile hike.	Sign up for Boy Scout hike	
Health	Avoid drugs unless prescribed by a doctor.	Stay away from those who do drugs; say no if offered.	

Making Good Choices Leads to Happiness

People who are happy have opted to be happy, but they also make decisions that lead to happiness. This is another key lesson about happiness that we strive to teach our children: good choices can lead to happiness. But how do you help children learn to make choices that will lead to their happiness? The answer is to provide questions they can ask themselves that will help them analyze their choices. Here are questions we teach our children to ask themselves when faced with a choice:

1. Will this hurt me or someone else?
2. Is it wholesome?
3. Is this right or wrong?
4. Do I need this or want this?
5. What are the consequences?

At our weekly Family Nights, we play a game to help practice making tough choices. We describe a real-life dilemma, consider the choices, and answer the questions above. Once these questions are answered, the decision that will lead to the most happiness becomes crystal clear. For example:

Dilemma:	*Choice #1:*	*Choice #2:*
You accidentally break a fun, but inexpensive, toy that your friend lent you.	Since the toy was not of great value, just say nothing and hope everyone forgets about it.	Admit that the toy broke and offer to replace it with something similar.
Decision-making Questions Will this hurt me or someone else?	I would hurt my friend by not being honest; I would be hurt because living with a lie is never easy.	This might be difficult to do, because admitting a mistake is never easy. However, I would not have to live with a lie.
Is it wholesome?	Neglecting to reveal something is close to lying and lying is not considered wholesome.	Telling the truth and admitting a mistake is wholesome.
Is this right or wrong?	Lying is not right.	Telling the truth is the right thing to do.
Do I need this or want this?	This question does not fit this situation, but applies when considering a purchase.	This question does not fit this situation, but applies when considering a purchase.
What are the consequences?	I would have to live with my conscience. In time, my friend might confront me about the missing toy and this might be awkward for both of us.	My friend and I would both learn a lesson about borrowing and lending possessions. The person who lends something must accept some risk, and the person who borrows something must accept some responsibility.

Experiencing Instead of Possessing Happiness

Phelecia: *Our daughter, who is in middle school, wears a ring with "CTR" engraved on it. These letters stand for the phrase, "Choose the Right," and they serve as a constant reminder to make wise choices whenever possible.*

Brent: *Years ago, when Phelecia and I had two kids and were living in a tiny apartment, we visited a wealthy friend at his estate. I asked him, "How did you get all this wealth? What is your key to your success and happiness?"*

"Don't make the same mistake I did," he said. "I gave my kids everything they wanted; I paid for it all. But I didn't give them what they needed—my time and attention. Forget wealth; if I could get my kids out of drug rehabilitation and have a normal life, that would be true happiness. I was so worried about getting rich, I lost what was really important, which was my kids. My wife and I are paying the ultimate price. My kids are unhappy. This is an unhappy place."

Movies, television shows, and magazines shout at us louder each day to buy more and more, so we will be happy. The goal of every advertisement is to convince us that our lives, status, and self-esteem will be improved by purchasing a certain product. When our children watch TV, listen to the radio, and read magazines, they are bombarded with "buy, buy, buy!" messages.

Spend time with your children and you can counteract the negative influence of the media. It sounds obvious, but it's true. By taking time to do anything with our children—read a book, take a walk, play sports, or work around the house—we demonstrate to them that experiences and relationships are more important than possessions. If we are good examples and a constant presence in their lives, we will be much more aware of danger signs indicating that our children might need our help. In addition, if we are a constant presence in their lives, our children will be more apt to come to us with their concerns and fears.

Our children are not materialistic partly because they must earn the things they want, but also because Brent and I do not focus on buying things that are bigger, better, and faster. We don't care about flashy clothes or cars. When our children see toys or "extras" they want, we have a simple response: "Work, save your money, and you can get it." This has taught them the value of money and work.

Teaching Financial Responsibility

Phelecia: *My middle son saved up $100 for a scooter he really wanted. He had used it for about a week when the motor burned out. It was going to be $300 to fix it and there was no warranty. He was upset and sad, but finally realized that sometimes you just get a "lemon." He then decided he wanted to earn money for a pogo stick and a unicycle, and thought it might be a good idea to buy them used instead of new because it wasn't as much money.*

When our children are about eight or ten years old, we give them a clothing budget and let them purchase their own clothes. We only provide guidance if the clothing is somehow indecent. Then we teach our kids to be savvy shoppers and to get good deals. They are excited when they get good deals just like Brent and I are. Even our teenager doesn't demand to have designer brand clothes and shoes most kids want, because he does not want to spend money needlessly. Our teenage daughters are the same way. They are excited to go to discount stores to buy clothes, because we have shown them the value of saving money.

Each child has a savings account and has seen how money can earn interest. Whenever they make money, we suggest they take out enough to have fun with, but save some as well. They have started begging us to take them to the bank to put their money into their savings accounts!

From an early age, we teach our children to donate a small portion of their earnings. Phelecia and I have always given 10 percent of our income to the poor. We model charity rather than greed, and our children have all developed a "soft spot" for the less fortunate. We think that by giving of themselves and their money, they will find true happiness.

The following 11 tips are from Dr. Severe, one of our favorite parenting experts. These ideas for teaching kids about money helped us show our kids the immediate results of having responsibility regarding money. These practices also helped them understand that money alone will not make them happy. They learned how giving money away can give us satisfaction and happiness. They also learned the sense of accomplishment that comes from managing money well.

1. *Explain the use of money.* Begin as early as age three. Show how things are bought and sold at the grocery store, toy store, etc. Children need to see the real-world use of money.
2. *Give children a weekly allowance.* Most parents have children earn their allowance through good behavior, responsibility, and household jobs. If you attach money to chores, be sure you don't get manipulated. Don't take away allowance as punishment.

   But we don't just hand over the money and let our kids do whatever they want with it. We make sure they budget their money just like we do. We give them each three envelopes, and here's why:

Strategy	***Purpose***
Label three envelopes with the following: 1. Money to spend 2. Money to save 3. Money for a good cause Each time your child has earned money, help him/her divide the money between the three envelopes. Discuss his/her plans for the money in each envelope.	Gives children a concrete example of how to manage their money. It helps them practice the values of thrift and charity.
Give older children a clothing budget and let them choose to spend it as they wish.	Teaches children responsibility with money.
Open a savings account for your child and show how the money earns interest.	Demonstrates how to save money and the positive consequences of doing so.

3. *Increase allowances as children grow.* Increasing responsibilities should result in increased allowance. Also, it is a good incentive to give extra allowance for extra work.
4. *Introduce expenses.* As allowance increases, the scope of expenses should widen. For example, teenagers should earn more allowance, but they should then have to use their allowance for dating and entertainment. Teens who insist on buying clothes with designer labels should pay the extra cost.
5. *Teach home budgeting.* Explain how a finite amount of money needs to be distributed for food, clothing, mortgage or rent, utilities, car expenses, etc. Include older children in family financial planning. Don't overprotect your children from this.
6. *Teach wise consumerism.* Have your children compare the same product in different size packaging to determine the best value. When children grow older, explain how and why you choose certain products. Compare prices at different restaurants. Teach about inflation by going to the library and reading about prices in old newspapers.
7. *Start a savings account.* Most children can comprehend the need for savings by age ten. Remember that children are naturally impulsive. In this age of advertising bombardment, children have a tendency to be impulsive spenders. Encourage your child to save a certain percentage of allowance. Some parents match savings.
8. *Start a checking account.* Some 16-year-olds are ready for a checking account and a limited credit card. You want them to learn how to manage these tools while you are still around to keep things from getting out of control.
9. *Set financial goals.* Discuss plans for paying for college. Have your high school students research scholarship and aid programs. Have them calculate tuition costs, living expenses, etc.

10. *Earn their own money.* The best way for children to learn about money is to get their own job as soon as they are old enough. Help them find a job that is safe, has reasonable hours, and includes friendly people.
11. *Moderation in all things—including moderation.* Children need to learn the value of money, how to earn it and how to manage it. But don't over do it. Spending money on something impractical once in a while is always fun.

What is Money Really Worth?

Phelecia: *The owner of an apartment we lived in became very wealthy, but never married or had a family. We were talking one day and he said, "I may have a lot of money, but you have so many gems: your children, your family, and your husband are your gems. I'm not truly happy, because I don't have anybody to share this with."*

We all define happiness differently, but one common element is fulfilling relationships with friends and family. Through these relationships we share the joys and sorrows of life's experiences, and by giving and receiving love we get the opportunity to embrace happiness that money cannot buy.

Qualities of Happy People

Happy people tend to have similar qualities; they are usually content, kind, compassionate, and warm. To be content, you need to be happy with who you are at each stage in your life, and be happy with what you have. We try to find happiness within ourselves in each moment of each day, and teach our children to find that same happiness.

Phelecia: *A few years ago, when we had four children, we had an opportunity to buy a home. It was only a one-bedroom, and so the children slept in one bedroom and we slept in the front room. I felt so blessed, and we were so excited to be homeowners.*

I remember some people said, "How do you fit in that little house? Why would you want to buy that little house? How can you be happy there?" They just went on and on, because our children slept in one bedroom.

Sometimes others' reactions can make it difficult to see the blessings in your own life. Where others saw an impossibly small house, we saw a blessing. It does not matter where you live; happiness is who you are.

Phelecia: *When I get upset or down, I count my blessings: my beautiful children who are all happy and healthy; our great country; our house; the food we eat; and a loving family.*

One way we help our family feel content is by being grateful. At your next family dinner or outing, have each person name five (or more) things for which they are grateful. Here is a list our children came up with at a recent family meeting:

Family Member	*"I am grateful for..."*
Shane	surfing, family, health, freedom, church
Chari	family, religion, health, talents, freedom
Ashlyne	family, home, talents, animals, religion
Mckay	family, sports, music, God, my mom and dad
Dakota	bugs, animals, family, God, my brothers and sisters
Saige	my mom, dad, sisters and brothers, flowers, home, God
Hunter	food, Spiderman, family, Jesus, my mom and dad

We do not judge our children for being grateful for TV shows or good food. The purpose of this activity is to feel content with what we have. Contentment is a natural antidote to greed, which is an unquenchable desire for more and more. To help our children avoid the pitfalls of greed, we help them appreciate what they have and feel the happiness that comes from contentment.

We also have found that in serving others we find true happiness. As parents, we care for and serve our children. In the community, we help the needy. When you help others, you lose yourself in a good way. The process of taking care of someone else brings us great joy and happiness, and if we get something in return, that is just a bonus.

Phelecia: *A neighbor said to me, "I've been watching you, and I just can't believe that you still have a smile on your face. How can you be so happy? Look at all your kids and all the responsibility you have! Why are you so happy all the time? Are you on Prozac?"*

If you are not happy, try doing things for others—open the door for someone or just smile! Lose yourself and take care of somebody else. It can't help but make you or someone else happy.

Phelecia: *I was in the grocery store and smiled at an older man, and he said, "I want to let you know how beautiful you are. So many people walk around with frowns on their faces, and I don't see a lot of people who are happy. You just glow with happiness, and I want to tell you, you just brightened my day."*

Embrace Happiness

Phelecia: *One of our daughters loves to smile at everybody, but if she smiles and does not get a smile in return, she gets so sad. She says, "I smiled at that person over there. How come she didn't smile back at me?"*

"You know, sometimes people can't do that," I remind her. "They can't always be happy, but you know, your beautiful smile helps so many people, so don't be offended if some people can't smile back."

Embrace happiness. Count your blessings. Be grateful. These sound like meaningless platitudes, but they are simple reminders of how to have a happy life and help your children along the same path. Brent and I have put a priority on family and on our spiritual life, and we make choices accordingly. These decisions are not always easy, but by living a life based on our priorities and values, we have achieved happiness. Take time to find noble (G-Rated!) goals, sound values, and wholesome pursuits. Then set your priorities and work towards them. Finally, find ten things you are happy about today.

CHAPTER 10

"I CAN!": TEACHING YOUR KIDS THE POWER OF POSITIVE THINKING

Brent: *When my brothers, sisters and I were young, my dad took an empty soda can and glued plastic eyes all over it. If we came to him and said we couldn't do something, he would point to the can and ask:*

"What kind of can is that?"

"It's a can," we'd answer.

"Yes, but what kind of can?"

"It's an 'eye can.'"

He would make us say "eye can" over and over until it sank in.

It is easy for us to forget how important it is to have an "I can!" attitude. If you think you can do something, eventually you will do it. If you think you cannot do something, you probably will not be able to do it. The more things you cannot do, the worse you feel about yourself, and the less you will be able to do. Soon you begin to feel useless and you stop trying. This is the negative, vicious cycle we want to avoid as adults and especially as parents. We believe that part of raising a G-Rated family is helping children adopt a positive "I can" attitude.

Brent: *We have signs on the walls in our house. They are in our bedroom, on the refrigerator, and in the bathroom. One says, "Attitude. Make it great. A bad attitude is like a dirty diaper. No one likes to be around it, but everyone wants to see it changed."*

It is funny, because when I have a bad attitude, get mad, or yell at the kids, or I am negative, the kids will point to the sign, and it reminds me to improve. It kind of irritates me sometimes, but it is my own doing. I know that by looking at my positive attitude signs constantly, I will have a positive attitude.

A positive attitude is very important when raising children, but we also realize that every person has trials in this life. We try to take those challenges and not let them paralyze us. It is easy to be drawn to self-pity and ask, "Why is this happening to me?" Try on the role of victor rather than victim. Look at trials, consider what you can learn from them, and meet them head on. Struggles will make us stronger if we don't let them tackle us.

If you are feeling negative most of the time, try this: choose your favorite quotes from the collection below, and write them on small note cards or print them out using your computer. Post them where you can read them every day. This may seem silly, but you are actually retraining your mind to think positively. Psychologists agree that our brain is wonderfully changeable and capable of learning new things and thought patterns even as we age.

Nothing can stop the man with the right mental attitude from achieving his goal. Nothing on earth can help the man with the wrong attitude.
–Thomas Jefferson

No one can make you feel inferior without your consent.
–Eleanor Roosevelt

There is nothing either good or bad, but thinking makes it so.
–William Shakespeare

Whether you think you can or think you can't, you are right.
–Henry Ford

We are what we think. All that we are arises with our thoughts. With our thoughts, we make the world.
–Buddha

Any fact facing us is not as important as our attitude toward it, for that determines our success or failure.
–Norman Vincent Peale

Twenty years from now you will be more disappointed by the things you didn't do than by the ones you did. So throw off the bowlines, sail away from the safe harbor. Catch the trade winds in your sails. Explore. Dream.
–Mark Twain

The Power of the Positive and the Pull of the Negative

Brent: *No one likes negative people. I don't. When I am negative, I don't like being around myself, and no one else likes to be around me. If you work on being positive, people will be drawn to you like a magnet. It's positive energy; it's good energy.*

Have you ever been to a party where the attitude is happy and everyone is having a good time? But all it takes is one negative person with a bad attitude and the energy can change completely.

Brent: *There was a lady who used to come over to our house, and she brought a negative atmosphere. You could cut it with a knife. Everything she said was so negative and she never saw the good in anybody. When she came over I wanted to leave. I couldn't* *stand it, and I would go in the back room. She would suck the life out of Phelecia. It took all of her energy to keep herself motivated because nothing made this woman happy.*

Having a positive attitude in your daily family life is very important. When kids see positive, happy parents each morning, they love it. It starts off the attitude for the day. They are getting ready to go to school, and they need that positive energy at home. They get enough negativity at school. Try to start each day with a positive word or gesture; it all begins in the home.

Phelecia: *I start each day with a cheerful greeting for each child. "How was your night? I'm glad to see you this morning."*

Sometimes we need help staying positive. Here are some things we have done:

1. Give yourself a reminder. Write yourself a note and put it on the bathroom mirror: "Today, I am going to be happy." "I'm going to smile at everybody this week."

2. Require yourself to say ten or 15 positive things each day.

3. Be positive just for today.

I think we all need practice looking for the good in people and situations. The glass can be half empty or half full; it's all about our attitudes.

A positive attitude makes your home a place where your child wants to be. If the energy in the home is positive, then everybody in the family wants to gather together. The parents are in control here; you know that old saying, "If I'm not happy, nobody is happy."

Try giving out as many compliments as you can, especially to your children. You will see an amazing transformation over time.

Brent: *When I was the head coach for my son's baseball team, I could only see what he couldn't do. "Son, you've got to hustle! Don't be a lazy player. Keep your eye on the ball. Concentrate on your swing." I doubt I ever said anything positive. Soon he dreaded practice, and he started talking about not liking baseball. I realized I had taken a kid who adored a sport and made him feel like a failure.*

So, for the next few games, I said only encouraging things and he started to improve, both in athletic ability and attitude.

Many parents fall into the same criticism trap I did, because they hope that they are helping their children learn the "right" way to do things. But when we focus on our children's strengths rather than their weaknesses, we make them feel good about themselves. When children feel good about themselves, they can do anything.

The media does not help girls feel good about themselves. Magazines, music videos, movies—you name the media outlet—tell girls and women that females must be thin and beautiful to be accepted. Studies even show that girls' self-esteem is lowered by 30 percent after looking at fashion magazines! We have struggled ourselves to understand how to raise girls who do not have eating disorders and who feel good about themselves and their bodies.

Phelecia: *When Brent and I were first married and before we had children, I was probably all of 115 pounds. But each time I would pick up a cookie or anything that you could possibly get heavy from, Brent would look at me and ask me if I really needed to eat that. I remember thinking, "Oh, my goodness," because I had never been exposed to that before.*

When I was young, I got a bit heavy. I had to wear larger sizes that were then called "pretty plus." Everyone knew it was a nice way of calling you plump. My parents handled it really well. They were never negative or critical. My mom and I did plan healthy meals together, and she often suggested we take walks.

Many parents try to control what, when, and how much their kids eat, but this strategy seems to backfire. There is something about human nature that makes us want to take that control back, because it is our body, no matter what. By being too rigid, negative, and controlling about food, parents can create eating disorders in their children.

There is also the feeling that your looks are not good enough, and, by extension, you are not good enough. This makes kids self-conscious.

So, I told Brent to let me figure out my weight and eating issues on my own. I assured him that it would be okay, unless he continued to tell me what I could and could not eat. That kind of thing would surely lead me to have eating problems. Brent said that was fine, he wouldn't bother me about it anymore, and he has always been very respectful.

***Brent:** I explained to Phelecia that in my family, my father scrutinized and criticized what my mother and sisters ate. Sometimes he would even weigh my mother or my sisters himself. If they didn't weigh the proper amount, then he refused to take my mother out to dinner or he wouldn't allow my sisters to go on a date.*

***Phelecia:** So Brent saw a terribly negative and abusive way to handle weight, eating, and body-image issues. He thought that was the way to handle the situation. He learned to leave me alone and let me figure it out on my own. It was wonderful that he had such an open mind.*

Our words and actions can make our children feel worthwhile and loved. If you have gotten into the habit of constantly criticizing or belittling your child, do the opposite! You can even tell your child you are trying to change the way you talk to him or her. Then slowly train yourself to notice what your child can do and mention those things.

Try Objectivity Rather Than Criticism

Try being a sportscaster rather than a critic. Here are some examples of how to interact with your child objectively rather than critically.

When your children experience failure, acknowledge their feelings, but help them understand that they will get through difficulties by working on the problem. Demonstrate for your children how to rise above things. When they come upon challenges, they won't give up and think they can't do it, but will know they can do it if they take it step by step and day by day. (Remember my father's "eye can!")

Situation	*Objective Response*
A young child is having difficulty putting a puzzle together.	"I see you have a puzzle piece and you're trying to make it fit. Now you are turning it and trying it another way; and turning it again to see if it fits. And it fits! How did you feel when the piece fell into place?"
An older child brings you a story he has written and wants your comments.	"Wow! You worked hard on this. How long did it take? What was your inspiration? What is your favorite part? I really could see, hear, and feel the part when__________. Are there any parts you would like to change?"
You've just finished watching your daughter's soccer game.	"What a game! I saw you dribbling, blocking, and passing. How did you feel about that goal you assisted with? I was amazed at how quickly you made that happen."
Your child shows you his artwork.	"Can you tell me about this? I see you used five different colors and many shapes and lines. What's your favorite part about it?"

Focus on the Positive

Brent: *I grew up in a big, religious family. Everyone had the perception that we were the perfect family, but we were not. Three months after Phelecia and I were married, my parents kicked us out of the family. Imagine getting married, and wanting the support of your parents, and then you are disowned. It was very painful.*

I think that my mom and dad did a great job raising us all, but when my siblings and I started to get older and make our own decisions about our marriages and careers, my dad felt a loss of control. They did not know what to do. As parents, we can appreciate wanting to continue to control our children and to try to keep them safe and happy. Unfortunately, my dad tried to regain control over his kids by telling them not to come around anymore.

Phelecia and I have struggled together to cope with our difficulties with my family. We try not to dwell on the negative; we say good things about the situation, and go on from there. We give it a positive spin. We live our own lives and try to be as emotionally healthy as we possibly can, so we can do the right thing for our children. We have learned from our parents' mistakes, will not repeat them, and we do the best we can with what we have.

Talking and writing about these issues is very therapeutic. Most people do not like talking about family problems, because they don't want people to know they have problems and perhaps think less of them. But we all have challenges, problems, or issues—whatever you want to call them. We all do.

Brent: *I think people worry about what other people are going to think. Who cares what other people think! I'm more concerned with what my son thinks about me than what someone down the street thinks. I'm more concerned with what my wife and my kids think about me and how they are.*

Every family also has a positive side. You take the positive things you have learned and use those strategies with your children. You look at the negative aspects and avoid doing those things! You make sure the positive things are the ones you incorporate in your parenting. This is easier said than done, but we hope each generation will learn from the next.

Phelecia: *Life is learning. As we parent, we try things, make mistakes, and then try again. It is so important that we help one another and validate one another instead of competing. We're all trying to raise good kids, but parenting is hard. I always feel better when someone reveals his or her difficulties, and I share mine. Then we don't feel so alone.*

It is not how you act, it is how you react that matters.

Phelecia: *One Saturday, I was busy getting ready for a bridal shower I was hosting for 50 women. I was baking and doing all the stuff that you do, and trying to get ready at the same time, and tend to the kids. I was all ready just in time, with not a hair or thread out of place.*

After everyone arrived I went in the kitchen to get some glasses. As I opened a cupboard, a bag of powdered sugar fell on my head. I was completely dusted from head to toe! I looked like I was about 100 years old because my hair was so gray.

I remember thinking, "Do I want to make this a positive or negative memory? Do I want to look back and laugh, or remember how mad and angry I got?"

How did it end? I didn't have time to take a shower, so I dusted myself off and headed out to the dining room and told all my guests what had happened. We all had a great laugh.

When you are in the midst of raising children, it seems that it will last forever, but really your time with them is short. As they get older, all you have is memories, and it is so important to have positive memories.

Chapter 11

"I Am Healed": Parenting with Courage and Conviction

"What gives you the energy and patience to raise seven children? We can barely handle two kids!" We hear comments like this one a lot from parents at seminars we teach or wherever we go with our seven children. Parents are eager for our parenting "secrets." Our seven children have helped us become better parents, and we do have some strategies, which we have shared. But something else drives us to be careful, concerned parents each and every day.

Brent and I have faced the bright and the dark experiences of our own childhoods. These experiences, as bad and as good as they were, have been blessings. These memories give us the conviction and the courage to make childhood a safe place for our children.

Phelecia: *My stepbrother was 16 when he came to live with our family. I was eight. He loved my long, silky hair. I insisted that my mother cut my hair. Weeks later, I took scissors and cut my stepbrother's face out of all the family pictures. I began begging not to be left alone with him.*

These were the ways my eight-year-old self tried to tell my parents that he was doing things to me that he should not. But as loving and careful as they were, my parents did not, could not understand. I could not make them know, because I didn't have the words with which to tell them.

Phelecia's loving family and strong faith helped her to cope with the abuse from her stepbrother. (He is presently in jail without parole for other crimes.) This experience has made both of us wary about who or what we allow in our household. We carefully "screen" the places and people our children visit. We are not naive about the world, and we are committed to giving our kids the skills to make it through the world safely. We make our children feel safe and loved, and then watch them blossom. Through this process, we feel our own childhood wounds heal.

Brent: *Growing up, everyone thought our family was perfect. At the time, I knew we were not perfect, but I also knew that my dad enjoyed the constant praise. I felt I needed to be perfect, and I hated it, but I did my best to please my parents.*

As a young man, I fell in love with and married Phelecia. As you have already heard, soon after our marriage, my parents disowned Phelecia and me. That was it. We were out of the family. For several years, I woke up each day feeling dead. My parents rejected me, and I was not sure how to carry on.

Brent did carry on, in spite of being disowned by his parents, and the experience made both of us understand the power of unconditional love. We love our own children unconditionally. They make mistakes and we love them; they drive us crazy and we love them. We will not turn them away or kick them out. We are conscious of how harmful it is to withhold love. We have not repeated what has gone on in many families, including Brent's, for generations. The love we have for our children has helped us cope with the loss of Brent's family. We still think about them and long to be one happy family. However, we have accepted that we cannot change how people feel about us. All we can do is love and care for those we treasure.

Like many folks in the world, we've been hurt and rejected by those we trusted most. Yet, it is the pain from those experiences that gives us unbounded energy and patience to parent our children as well as we can. We cannot undo the past, but we can face it and take steps to protect our family's future. That is how parenting has helped us heal emotional wounds.

Chapter 12

"Help!": G-Rated Answers to Real-Life Questions

This chapter is a collection of questions we are frequently asked at our seminars. When Brent and I do not have the answer, we find an expert who does. Here are some of our favorite questions and answers—from our own experiences and from our favorite parenting experts.

Taming Temper Tantrums

My child throws a temper tantrum whenever we go out in public. I don't want to go out anymore. It makes me angry. How can we stop the tantrums?

Kids and temper tantrums go hand in hand; we've all been through them! When that's happened with our children, we actually take them out of the store (or restaurant, or wherever it may be) and let them know that their actions are unacceptable and if they keep it up we're going to go home. Also, what really helps is if you talk to them ahead of time and tell them that if they can make it through this trip then they can have some kind of treat. Talk to them ahead of time about the treat and let them pick out a certain thing so that they understand what you expect from them. A lot of parents give their children treats to make them stop acting up and the child learns very quickly to act badly to get what he wants.

On the other hand, if you only reward the good behavior that is how they will behave to get what they want.

Enjoying Your Children

How can we enjoy being parents even when our children misbehave and challenge us in other ways?

You cannot accuse children of being boring. They will always think of something you are unprepared to handle. Being a parent is demanding. Parenting requires countless sacrifices and continuous hard work. Fortunately, there are many rewards: the pride of achievement, the miracle of growth and development; warmth and affection. If your children's misbehavior is depriving you of these rewards, you are being cheated. Do not let their misbehavior interfere. You are doing the work without the glory. You are being denied the pleasures of parenting. You deserve to enjoy your children.

All parents want to enjoy their children. Few parents get the enjoyment they deserve. It is easy to appreciate your children when they are cooperative and well behaved. You can spend your time and energy on pleasant endeavors. You do not have to yell and argue. It is difficult to enjoy your children when they misbehave. Misconduct creates tension.

Many parents avoid their children to escape the stress and irritated feelings. They send their children outside to play so they do not have to deal with them. They cannot wait until the children go to bed. They see their children as a burden and resent them. They hope for the day when their children leave home. This is a tragic waste of a precious opportunity.

Being a successful parent is hard work. Developing well-behaved children requires courage and patience. Trust yourself. You know what is best for your children. Concentrate on the real issues: mental health, happiness, self-respect, and love of others.

Some parents believe that love alone will create delightful children. Love is essential, but it does not guarantee good behavior. Misbehavior is not pleasant. There is a better way. You have a right to enjoy being a parent. Do not let your children's misbehavior keep you from enjoying them. Take action. Plan to change the misbehavior and then have fun. Laugh and play and get involved with your children. It will keep you feeling young. These are the most valuable years of your life.

Keeping Up with Bobby

My son wants things that his friends have and we don't have the money. What should I do?

All kids want what their friends have. We suggest that they go out and work and earn the money. This teaches kids to respect money and work. Money doesn't provide happiness and children don't always understand that. But you can help them develop a plan to earn the money they need by working. That can really help open their eyes to how much things cost.

Considering Sleepovers

We don't allow our kids to spend the night at other people's houses, and they get really upset. They feel as if they are missing out. What should we do?

Phelecia and I have a very strict policy about sleepovers. We have good reason to be cautious. When Phelecia was 12, she had a friend named Leslie Berry. One day after school Leslie suggested swimming at her apartment. Phelecia's mom was working at the time and so Phelecia always had to call her and check in. Phelecia's mom asked who would supervise the girls and then would not let Phelecia go swimming when she found out the apartment manager would be taking care of them. Phelecia's mom said that she didn't have a good feeling about it. Phelecia was angry and disappointed, and Phelecia's friend left. About a week later Phelecia found out that Leslie had been murdered by the apartment manager, who had also been molesting her.

As parents, we all have instincts and feelings about what is right and wrong for our children and it is so important for us to listen to these feelings. To this day, Phelecia is grateful that her mom followed her instincts.

As for your situation, take time to explain your sleepover policy to your kids. Your reasons might not be as dramatic as ours, but they are just as valid. Then offer other suggestions: the child or teen can come spend the night at your house; or your child can go over to a friend's house and stay until 10:30 p.m. Try to find a solution whereby you can meet each other half way. Sometimes the children are going to be upset and not want to do what you ask them, but you are the parent and at some point, we hope, they will understand that.

Heading Off Homework Hassles

What can parents do to make homework less of a hassle for the whole family?

Homework is one of the greatest sources of conflict between children and parents. Children avoid doing homework. They procrastinate until the last minute. They fail to bring it home. They make excuses. They do as little as possible. They take too long. They do it too fast. They do not do their best. Parents become frustrated and angry with these attitudes and behaviors. The source of this frustration is often disappointment. We want our children to do well in school. Parents become embarrassed when children perform poorly on their homework. They wonder, "What will the teacher think of me?"

Most parents realize the value of homework. Most children do not. Parents know that homework reinforces skills.

Practice makes perfect. Children see homework as repetitive and busywork. Parents know that children who do quality homework learn more and get better grades. Some children see homework as a penalty for not getting everything done at school.

Parents and teachers need to be partners in the development of healthy homework habits in children. Teachers need to explain the value of homework to their students. Teachers need to explain that homework is to help the students learn. It impacts their grades and their futures. Homework develops responsibility, independence, and accountability. It develops personal organization skills and teaches children to manage their time.

Your job as a parent is to be a homework facilitator. There are several factors to consider when developing successful homework strategies. Visit or call your child's teacher and ask about his or her homework policy. How often will homework be given? How much homework will there be? What subjects? Ask to be notified in advance when special projects are due. When are the tests? Will there be study guides? This information will enable you to develop a better homework plan.

Children need to know that doing homework is their job not yours. Many parents have to stand over their children each night. Every assignment is a struggle. Homework is between your child and his teacher. You are only a facilitator. Your job is to help — not do it for him. Do not make this mistake. If you are already trapped in this dilemma, stop tonight. Tell your child that your responsibility is to help. His responsibility is to complete the homework. Here is what you can do to help:

Homework Time

Be sure your child has enough time to do homework. Children are involved in many activities: athletics, music lessons, dance class, scouts, and church clubs. These are excellent, but homework must be the priority. Have a set time for homework each day. Negotiate this time with your children, if possible. Reschedule around other activities only when necessary. Check with your child's teacher to determine how much time will be needed. If your child has no homework, he can read from his favorite book for 30 minutes. The same is true for a child who "forgets" his homework. These techniques let children know that homework is important.

Homework Place

Have a specific place to do homework. This place should be distraction free. Turn off the TV during homework time. Parents can set an example by reading. Be sure your child has a table and chair. The kitchen table works fine, as long as there is quiet. Be sure there is adequate lighting. Have all necessary supplies nearby so that homework time is not spent hunting for glue or tape or paper. Your child's teacher can give you a list of items to put into a supply box. Older children may need a calculator and, eventually, a computer.

Homework Strategy

Some children resist doing homework. The first thing to do is to be sure the child can do the homework. Check with the teacher. If ability is not the problem, it may be that your child sees the assignment as overwhelming. Break the assignment into more manageable parts. This promotes success. Preview the assignment with your child. Read the directions and check for understanding. Do the first question or problem with your child. This will let him know that, while it may seem difficult at first, he can do it. Provide encouragement at each step. "You do the next three on your own and then I'll come back and check them." Tell your child that you have confidence in his ability to complete the work and do his best. "You did the first one correctly, I bet you can do the next three and get them all right." Be available to answer questions.

Another strategy is to teach children to do the worst first. If your child has difficulty with math, have them do it first. They will get it over and will feel relieved. The remaining assignments will be less threatening. Doing the worst first makes more sense because your child is more alert mentally.

Homework Revelance

Some children resist doing homework because they question the relevance of the assignment. "Why do I have to do that? It's stupid." "I did this last year; I am not doing it again." Unfortunately, not every assignment has equal meaning to every child. Some assignments may be irrelevant and boring. These assignments must be done anyway. Tell them, "You do not have to like it, but you have to do it." This is how the real world operates. We all have aspects of our jobs that are irrelevant and boring. We get used to it.

Homework Buddy

Students in fourth grade and up can benefit from having a homework buddy. Have your child get the phone number of a friend in each class. If your child has difficulty, forgets an assignment, or is sick for a day, he can call the buddy and get information and help. Older students should be taught to use a homework organizer. Many schools have them for sale.

Homework Accuracy

Some children speed through their assignments. This is only a problem if the work is sloppy or inaccurate. If the work is neat and correct, homework is finished for the day. Do not penalize your child for working quickly, as long as he is accurate. If the work is sloppy or inaccurate, have your child redo the assignment. If you anticipate that your child may be a speeder, let him know your rules ahead of time.

Homework Incentives

For most children, the organization and planning strategies discussed above, along with some verbal encouragement, are enough to get successful homework habits started. For some children these tactics are not enough. Some children are reluctant. Some children dawdle. These children need stronger incentives.

Use computers and educational software to motivate your children. There are hundreds of software programs that reinforce reading, spelling, and math skills. There are interactive encyclopedias, history, and science programs. There are on-line research services. These kinds of learning tools are fun and exciting.

Checklists, charts, and contracts are good motivators. Have daily, weekly, or long-term pay-offs. Make a list of the specific activities that your child must follow in order to improve homework habits.

Use a checklist to emphasize the importance of taking responsibility. Children must realize that school success and doing homework is for them, not you. You already have your education. They need to learn to do well in school to please themselves, not you.

Punishment does not motivate children to do better in school. Punishment does not motivate children to do their best on homework. You can not make your child learn. Motivation to learn and do school work can only be achieved through encouragement and self-discipline. Avoid homework power struggles. Arguments over homework only provide your children with another button to push.

Motivating Kids

How can parents motivate children?

My son won't do anything.

What do you mean?

All he does is watch TV.

Does he have any responsibilities around the house?

Yes. But getting him to do them is a struggle. Everything is a struggle.

How does he do in school?

He passes. He could do better if he worked a little. He is so unmotivated.

We hear comments like these from parents often. Yet we are convinced that all children are motivated. Not all children are motivated to behave and work hard. Some children are motivated to do nothing.

Think about motivation in two ways. Some motivation comes from inside you — it is internal. Some motivation comes from outside you — it is external. Being overweight is bad for your heart. Losing weight to improve your health requires internal motivation. You have to have a desire to lose weight. Losing weight to win a bet is an example of external motivation.

Most of us get up and go to work each day for two reasons. We get personal satisfaction from our work — internal. We also get paid — external. We need both. Most of us do not drive at 100 miles per hour. We know it is unsafe — internal. We do not want to go to jail — external. Internal and external motivation work together to produce a responsible person.

Emphasize Success

Success creates internal motivation. When your boss praises your work, you feel successful and continue to work hard. You can use success to give your child a boost of internal motivation. Point out your child's good behavior and decisions. Your child will feel successful. Success motivates him to work harder. When you compliment your child for having a clean bedroom, he will feel good inside — he will feel successful. He will be more motivated to keep his room clean.

Many children believe they cannot be successful. This false belief usually comes from repeated failures. Sometimes it is the result of high expectations. Correct this problem by spotlighting the positive. Point out strengths. Show your child where he has made progress. Encourage him to believe in himself. This will help your child feel success. Once success gets started, it continues. Success breeds success.

Develop expectations that build on success. This strategy is called "shaping." When you are teaching a complex behavior, divide the task into small sequential steps. Expect progress not perfection. Consider this example:

> Liz would like to teach her son, Carlos, how to get ready for school. This includes getting washed, brushing his teeth, getting dressed, and making his bed. Liz decides that getting washed by himself has first priority. It may take a few days or a few weeks before Carlos becomes proficient at washing. Once accomplished, Liz teaches Carlos to brush his teeth and get dressed. Finally, Liz teaches Carlos to make his bed.

The small sequence of steps improves the probability of success. Placing all the tasks on Carlos would have been unreasonable. It may have resulted in frustration and failure. Shaping takes time. It is a good method of teaching.

Use shaping to improve behavior gradually. Shaping means encouraging better effort. Suppose your child takes 40 minutes to do a chore that should take ten minutes. Set a timer and play "Beat the Clock." Praise him for completing the job within the limit. Starting with a time limit of ten minutes may cause failure. To improve the chances for success, start with a time limit of 30 minutes. This is still an improvement over 40 minutes. After a week, move the limit to 25 or 20 minutes. Gradually, you will achieve the ten-minute goal. Shaping improves the chance of successful behavior.

When teaching new expectations, reinforce improvements or steps in the right direction. Do not insist on perfect performance on first attempts. Just because you have taught your five-year-old how to make his bed, do not expect him to do the job as well as you. He will be happy with a lumpy bedspread at first. He will steadily improve with your guidance and encouragement.

A child who misbehaves frequently lacks the internal motivation to cooperate. Use praise and encouragement to get success started. Once he experiences good behavior, he will be more motivated to behave in the future. Tell your child when he is doing well. That will motivate him further.

Parents have a tendency to focus on negative behavior. We tell our children what they are doing wrong. Misbehaviors get our attention. Many parents believe that being critical of mistakes is one way to instill more effort on the part of the child. This is not true. Focus on what your children do well.

Your son does a mediocre job sweeping the garage. "You didn't sweep the corners at all. You're so lazy. A six-year-old could do better." This type of criticism is not motivating. This is better. "You got the middle part okay. You missed some dirt in the corners. I'll do one corner to show you how. Then you can do the rest. Do the corners as well as you did the middle and it will look great." This comment is encouraging. It builds success. Success motivates children to work harder.

At times, you may need incentives that are stronger than praise and encouragement. Incentives can be an allowance, toys, or privileges. Use charts and contracts. Make an agreement with your child. "Have a good week in school and we will do something special on Saturday." Children like working toward a goal. Do not set the standards too high. This can create too much pressure and have a reverse effect on motivation. Do not expect perfect behavior for two months before you allow your daughter to go to the movies. You are expecting too much.

Whenever you use incentives such as rewards or privileges, always accompany the incentive with verbal encouragement. Always remind your child that the reason to behave and work hard is to feel good about yourself. Aim for self reward. That is always more important than the actual incentive.

> *I hope you feel good about your week in school. You should be proud of yourself. A little hard work really pays off. I'm glad you earned the movie on Saturday. But, I hope you understand that the best reason to do well in school is you. Do well in school because it is good for you. You are more important than the movie.*

Use Interest

Interest creates motivation. Suppose that you are trying to improve your child's reading skills. You know that your child likes dinosaurs. By reading books about dinosaurs, you will increase your child's motivation. Your child's interest in dinosaurs makes the reading meaningful and fun. Your child is motivated to learn because he is interested in what he is reading.

Make learning interesting. With young children, you can make changes in a child's behavior by playing a game. Pat taught her daughter, Katie, how to make her bed by playing role reversal. Katie played the mom and the mom played the child. Katie liked being the mother, so making the bed became a fun-filled activity.

Family Climate

A pleasant family climate motivates children. Family climate refers to the way everyone in the family feels about each other. Pleasant family climate develops in families in which members speak politely to each other and discipline is positive. Everyone feels a sense of togetherness and cooperation. Structure is balanced with flexibility. Everyone is encouraged to pursue his or her own interests. The family has fun together; they have inside jokes. When the climate is warm and accepting, children learn your values and goals. Children are willing to accept guidance and punishment because they see that you are acting out of love and concern. If a problem occurs, the children will rebound more quickly.

Unpleasant family climate develops in families in which there is anger and criticism. The rules and structure are rigid — there is no room for individual flexibility. Everyone becomes defensive. The parents see more bad than good. The children are always picking on each other.

Family climate begins with parents who are good models. Teach your children to thank people who are nice to them. Teach them to apologize to those they hurt. Teach them to be empathetic. Teach them to comfort others who are not doing well. The best way to teach these qualities is by living them yourself. Do not complain about helping Grandma with her shopping. Explain that helping others makes you feel good inside — that's the reward.

Make your children feel secure and safe. Children like everything in the family to run smoothly. Children worry about changes. Children worry about changes at school. They worry when Dad gets a new job. Explain changes before they happen. Reassure your children that you will always love them.

Look for family climate the next time you go shopping. Find a place to sit and watch families. When you see a family walking together and talking nicely to one another, you are looking at pleasant family climate. If you hear the parents say, "Stand up straight when you walk. Hold on to that package, I don't want to lose it. Walk over here with us," you are looking at unpleasant family climate. If you hear the children say, "I'm telling.

You're in trouble. Tell her to stop teasing me. Look what he is doing, Mom," you are looking at unpleasant family climate.

Pleasant climate can be disrupted by a negative situation, such as an argument between two children. If a situation creates an unpleasant family climate, put it behind you. Change the subject. Think of something positive. Return to a pleasant family climate as soon as possible. If two of your children have an argument, help them reach a settlement. Then redirect their energy. You may need to stay with them for a while to ensure better feelings toward each other. Go for a walk. Read a story. Get them involved in something pleasant.

Family climate can fluctuate. Some days the climate is pleasant; other days it is not. This is normal. Aim for more good days than bad days. If one parent promotes a pleasant climate and the other does not, the children will adjust. Make your time with the children pleasant. Some pleasant climate is better than none.

The Benefit of Humor

One important aspect of pleasant family climate is humor. Humor can redirect family climate. When everyone is feeling down, a little humor helps turn things around. Humor can also redirect misbehavior. This works especially well with young children. "Is that your Grinch face? What happened? What turned your smile face into a Grinch face?" If your child is familiar with the story of Snow White, you can make comparisons to Grumpy and Happy.

You can also use humor for occasional forgetfulness. Your child forgets to sweep the patio. Leave him a note. "I hope you have a nice day on the PATIO!" You may want to tape the note to the broom handle and set it by his bedroom door. This only works well if your child has honestly forgotten. If he "forgot" because he did not feel like sweeping the patio, humor is not appropriate. Discipline and consequences are appropriate.

Not all mischief is misbehavior. Children can get into plenty of trouble without intending misbehavior. Mary had four young children. One day, the middle two wanted to be mommy's helpers. Mom was busy with an ill baby. So they decided to wash the kitchen tile. They had seen Mom wash the tile before. They were sure they knew what to do. One went for the mop and pail while the other went for the vinegar. They had seen Mom use vinegar to clean the floors. Mary heard the commotion in the kitchen. She put the baby down. She hurried to see what was happening. When her first foot hit the kitchen floor, it slid out from under her. She slid halfway across the floor. Next to the vinegar, Mary kept the olive oil. At least she used to.

Summary

Point out things your children do well. This makes them feel successful. Success encourages children to be more motivated. Interesting activities encourage children to enjoy learning. Maintaining a pleasant family climate helps children develop cooperation. These factors increase motivation, improve decision-making, and promote good behavior.

Make a list of activities you can do to create and maintain a pleasant family climate. Here are some ideas to get you started:

- Play games
- Read stories
- Tell jokes
- Go for a walk and talk
- Have discussions at the dinner table
- Be helpful to each other
- Listen to music
- Practice giving compliments to each other

Rewarding Good Behavior

How do you suggest rewarding children for good behavior?

Joey decides to stop associating with Tim. He has decided that Tim gets in too much trouble. Joey's parents praise his decision. "That took a lot of courage. It shows you are thinking for yourself. Growing up isn't always easy. You seem to be handling it quite well. We are proud of you. We hope you are proud of yourself."

Tiffany runs up to her mother. "My room is clean, Mom. Come and take a look." Mom examines the room. "Great job, Tiffany. You should be proud of yourself. Your room looks very neat."

Joey's parents and Tiffany's mom are using positive feedback. They are looking for good decisions. They are pointing out the things their children are doing well. It is like shining a spotlight on good behavior.

Positive feedback is the most powerful tool you have to improve your children's behavior and self-esteem. Positive feedback is a pay-off for good behavior. Positive feedback means using praise or incentives to encourage good decision-making. Positive feedback is not something new, but we often forget to use it. If you desire better behavior from your children, increasing your awareness and use of positive feedback is essential.

How to Use Positive Feedback

You can use positive feedback in two ways — to increase desirable behavior or decrease undesirable behavior. Using positive feedback to strengthen a desired behavior is easy. Simply look for a good behavior. When it occurs, reinforce it. When your children are well behaved, reward them with a few words of praise or encouragement, a hug, or a privilege.

You would like your children to share with each other. When your children share something, reinforce the sharing.

You could say: "I like the way you are sharing." "I see you have decided to share your toys this morning. That's a good decision." "I am proud of the way you are sharing the TV. That shows you are growing up. Good for you!"

Positive feedback is simple to use. The difficult part is remembering to look for the good behavior. Often, we only see the misbehavior in our children and take good behavior for granted. Be proactive. Strengthen good behavior by telling your children you appreciate it. Focus on the positive aspects of your children's behavior. That takes practice. If you increase your use of positive feedback, even if you make no other changes in your parenting behavior, your children will start making better decisions.

Replacement

You can also use positive feedback to eliminate or weaken misbehavior. This technique works with patterns of misbehavior, not misbehavior that is staring you in the face. First, determine the misbehavior. Next, determine the opposite behavior. Six-year-old Nathan argues and fights with his four-year-old sister, Ashley. The opposite of this misbehavior occurs when Nathan is playing nicely and cooperating with Ashley. Praise Nathan for playing nicely. Playing cooperatively will replace fighting. He will learn a more acceptable way of playing. "You are helping your sister draw. Good for you." The arguing and fighting will occur less often. This is a simple but effective strategy. Use positive feedback to strengthen the opposite behavior. The original misbehavior will decrease.

Most parents see the value in using positive feedback. It is common sense. There are some parents who resist the use of rewards and incentives. Whenever we face this concern, we explain how children are motivated. Many children are self-motivated to be well behaved and cooperative. This is not the case with all children. Positive feedback gives children a motivation boost. It builds self-esteem. Positive feedback encourages children to be more self-motivated.

Adults need positive feedback, too. Paychecks are an example of positive feedback. Your self-motivation would not keep you at work if you were not paid. This is how our society operates. The sooner children learn this idea the better. Parents who object to using rewards must remember that their goal is to have children who make good decisions. Not all children are self-motivated to achieve this goal. Using positive feedback gets things going in the right direction. Then self-motivation takes over.

Aim for Self Reward

Use positive feedback that teaches your child to value himself. "You made the right choice because you knew it was the correct thing to do." It is all right for children to behave and work hard to please their parents. It is better when they behave and work hard for themselves.

I like the way you did that. (Good)

Well done. You should be proud of yourself. (Better)

The second statement creates a sense of success and self-value. It is aimed at building self-esteem. Whenever you reward your child with an incentive, such as an allowance, add a comment that causes your child to think about doing the right thing. "You did a wonderful job on your chores. Here's your allowance. I hope you feel good about yourself."

Children Believe What You Tell Them

Children act the way you expect them to act. If you tell your son that he is noisy, he will live up to that expectation. If you tell your son that he knows how to play quietly, he will live up to that expectation. When you put a t-shirt on a child that says "Here Comes Trouble," you are encouraging your child to think of himself as a troublemaker. Here is what many parents say to teenagers who have messy bedrooms.

> *I do not understand why you're so sloppy. Look at this mess. What's wrong with you? You can't even keep your closet straight. Aren't you ashamed? When was the last time you made this bed? You'll never change.*

What is the parent saying? "You are a slob. That's why your room is a mess. You will always be a slob. That's what I expect from you. I am giving up hope of any improvement."

Here is the same teenager, same bedroom, different message.

> *You know, Tina, this is not like you. You are a neater person than this. I know you can be tidy. I know you have pride in yourself. I'm sure you can do better in the future. Don't you think so, too?*

Here is what the parent is saying. "I trust you. I have confidence in you. You can do better. Do it for your own sake." Your child will not make radical changes overnight, but you will be planting a healthier seed in his mind.

Be specific when you praise your children. Praise the behavior, not your child. "Your room looks great. It looks like you worked hard. I hope you are proud." Do not say, "You are such a good boy for cleaning your room." This has a double message. Is your son not good when his room is messy? Be generous with praise and encouragement, but use it wisely. Undeserved praise can lead to conceit or false confidence. Do not tell your child he has worked hard if he has not.

By praising specific behavior, you clearly indicate correct decision-making. You call attention to strengths. This gives your child confidence. He will feel capable of making good decisions.

Children need encouragement, especially children with poor self-esteem and children who lack persistence and determination. Encouragement gives children a boost of motivation. It helps them through difficult situations. It helps them face fears and withstand stress. It helps them solve problems and feel successful. Encouragement provides support, trust, and belief.

Tell your child that you love and value him. Accept your child for what he is, not for what he does. Show trust and confidence in your child's abilities and decisions. Recognize effort and improvement.

Summary

Children believe what you tell them. Children act the way you expect them to act. If you focus on positive qualities you will build stronger positive qualities. Use praise and encouragement that teaches your children to value themselves.

We once saw a poster with a child looking rather discouraged. The caption read, "When I mess up, no one forgets. When I do well, no one sees." Positive feedback is easy to use, but we often forget. Retrain yourself to look for the positive qualities in your children. Look for good decisions. Spotlight good behavior.

Earning Special Activities

I give my kids treats occasionally, but lately I feel as though they take the treats for granted. How can I change this behavior?

Wise parents connect special activities to good behavior. About ten years ago, we spent a few days with some friends from high school. They have three children of various ages. One evening, we all piled into their van and went out for ice cream. Later that night, after the children had all gone to bed, we began talking about being parents. Our friends asked if we had any suggestions for them. We said, "Never give away the ice cream."

We explained that at no time was any connection made between their children's behavior that day and our trip for ice cream. Successful parents connect special events to good behavior. "You have had an excellent day today. Mom and I would like to take you out for some ice cream." You can be more specific: "I saw you sharing several times today. That's something that makes Mom and me feel fantastic. When we feel good, we feel like doing something special."

We are not suggesting that we stuff sweets in our children's mouths whenever they are well behaved. We advise most parents to avoid sweets in favor of special activities. There are many ways to make the connection between having a good day and special events: going out for dinner, going to a movie, or even going for a Sunday afternoon drive. What about days when behavior has not been so good? Do not go out for ice cream on bad days.

We have always found that teachers who are good disciplinarians use this idea instinctively. These teachers make statements such as, "Danny, you worked hard on math this morning, please take this note to the office for me." "Jill, you really helped Jason with his reading, please help me hand out these papers." We once observed a teacher who said, "Beth, you have been pleasant to work with this afternoon. I'd like you to stay at the end of the line and shut the lights off when we go to art class." This clever teacher made a privilege out of being last in line.

Children love special activities. That's why special activities are such powerful incentives for good behavior. Playing computer games, talking on the telephone, and going out with friends are examples of activity incentives. Use activity incentives this way: first you work, and then you play. "Clean your room before you play video games." "Do your homework before you play outside." Do not get trapped by promises. "I will study after the movie."

Always add an encouraging comment when your child earns an activity. "I hope you feel good about earning extra skateboard time." Emphasize feeling good about yourself, not the skateboard time. Enhance activities by becoming involved. Playing a game is fun. Playing a game with a parent is more fun. There are also special privilege activities such as staying up late.

Be careful not to dangle every little activity in front of your children's noses. That will give them the wrong idea. You do not want them to think they have to be perfect. They will resent you for this and develop a poor attitude about working toward goals. Allow some fun activities to happen routinely. You also do not want them to think that every time they behave, you have to come up with a special reward. Children need to learn that good behavior is important because it is the right thing to do.

Tangible incentives are things children want. Examples are food, toys, CDs, money, etc. Tangible incentives work best when they are accompanied with words of thanks and encouragement. "Here's your allowance, Sue. You did a great job on your chores this week. Good for you."

We suggest making a menu of activities or treats tailored to your children's own likes and interests. Use the "How Well Do You Know Your Child?" survey on page 47 as a guide. When your children make good choices, behave well, or simply have a good day, bring out the menu. Let your children choose an activity from the menu as their incentive. This builds better decision-making skills and creates stronger self-esteem. Enjoy your ice cream.

Establishing and Enforcing Rules

Parenting books and magazines suggest using rules to help children learn self-discipline. But I have trouble enforcing the rules I have set. What is your advice?

Rules tell your children how you want them to behave. Rules are expectations, and they guide children's decision-making. There are three factors to consider when developing expectations or rules: expectations must be specific, reasonable, and enforceable.

Expectations Must Be Specific

Expectations are specific when they communicate precisely what your child should or should not do. Most parents do not give their children clear and specific expectations. They say, "Clean your bedroom once a week." This is not specific. Here is a specific expectation:

Please clean your bedroom every Saturday morning before noon.

Checklist:

- *All dirty clothes put in the laundry basket.*
- *All furniture dusted and polished.*
- *Sheets changed.*
- *All toys in toy box.*
- *All clean clothes put away.*
- *Carpet vacuumed.*

Look at your expectations from your child's point of view. "Clean your room" can be vague and unclear. The task may look impossible to your child. A checklist gives your child exact steps to do — one at a time — and lets them know exactly when they have fulfilled your expectations.

Expectations Must Be Reasonable

Can your child accomplish the tasks you expect? The above checklist is specific, but it is unreasonable for a three-year-old. You can expect a young child to keep clothes and toys put away, but not dust and vacuum or change the sheets.

Expectations Must Be Enforceable

You can see when your child's bedroom is clean. The checklist is enforceable. Many parents have expectations that are not enforceable. This occurs often with teenagers. "You may never associate with Nicole again." This rule is not enforceable. You cannot follow your daughter around school. You cannot control all the places your daughter may associate with Nicole. It would be more enforceable to restrict Nicole from coming to your home. "You may not invite Nicole to our home."

A few, well-developed rules and expectations are better than many poorly developed ones. Have a set of rules. Have a rule for cooperation, listening the first time, or following directions. Have a rule for morning and evening routines. Have a rule about chores. Have a rule about homework time.

Keep in mind that, just like discipline, rules are our friends. Children crave rules just as they want discipline. Do you want to be more consistent? Clear, simple rules will ensure that you are consistent. In addition, they help you focus on priority behaviors.

Consequences Teach Decision-Making

Children earn positive consequences for choosing to follow rules. They earn negative consequences for not following rules. Consequences teach children how to make decisions. Good decisions result in positive consequences. Poor decisions result in negative consequences. Consequences teach children that there is cause-effect in the world. They begin to internalize this thought: "This is what happens when I choose this behavior."

Consequences must also be specific, reasonable, and enforceable. A consequence is specific when the child knows exactly what is going to happen and is able to understand, "If I choose this action, this will be the result." Consequences are reasonable when they make sense. Most parents are more reasonable when they are not angry.

Consequences must be enforceable. Choose consequences that you control. A physician asked for our advice. He promised his 12-year-old "anything he wanted" if he made the school honor roll. The boy made the honor roll and asked for a dune buggy. We told Dad he got off easy. The kid could have asked for a Porsche. Do not promise things you cannot deliver just to excite your child's motivation.

At one seminar, a mother told her story from adolescence. Her father promised her a car if she improved in school. She explained how she remembered feeling. "Am I so bad and lazy that my father has to offer me a car to do better?" Her father's offer was well intended. It backfired. Promising a car was overdoing it. It was too much. It made her feel worse. It did not encourage her.

"It's Your Decision"

Use rules and consequences to teach your children that behaving in a responsible manner is their choice. Their choices determine their consequences; you do not.

"Stephanie, I would like you to be home for supper every day by five o'clock. I will trust you to be on time. You have shown a lot of responsibility lately. This will be an opportunity to prove your maturity." Mom gives Stephanie an incentive for being home on time. "If you are home on time, you can stay up an extra half hour and go out and play the next day." Mom explains the punishment. "If you choose to be late, you will go to bed at your regular time and not have play time the next day. It's your decision." Stephanie agrees.

When Stephanie is home on time, Mom compliments her. If Stephanie comes home late, Mom could say, "I'm really sorry you were late, Stephanie. It's too bad you will miss the last half-hour of your favorite show tonight. I really wanted you to see it."

Notice how this plan puts the responsibility on Stephanie, not Mom. Mom is still a nice person. She is on Stephanie's side. Stephanie makes the choice to go to bed early when she chooses to be late. Once expectations and consequences are set, stick to them. Be consistent. Be flexible before you establish expectations, not after an infraction.

Reality Consequences

Reality consequences occur naturally. A child who refuses to eat dinner goes hungry. A child who refuses to wash will develop body odor. When schoolmates begin commenting, the youngster will begin washing. Reality consequences also have positive results. A child who studies earns good grades. A child who does his chores earns an allowance. A youngster who exercises feels healthy. Reality consequences teach responsibility and decision-making because they permit children to learn from the real world. Use reality consequences whenever possible.

When expectations are too difficult, children become discouraged. Do not expect perfection. When expectations are too easy, children take advantage. Expectations are appropriate when children have to put forth effort without frustration.

Behavior is a choice. Tell your children how you expect them to behave. Then follow through with appropriate consequences. Be consistent with this technique and your children will make better decisions. They will choose responsible behavior.

Planning for Good Behavior

Is there a way to stop misbehavior before it starts?

With a little planning and thought, you can prevent misbehavior before it starts. We call this being proactive, but it really just means planning ahead. Life is easier when you plan ahead. Many discipline problems can be avoided with a little planning. Planning makes use of the only advantage that we have over our children: experience. We are not more intelligent. They have more time and certainly more energy. If you plan, you will have fewer problems.

Anticipate

Suppose you are taking your children out for pizza. You know the restaurant will be crowded. There are many video games and other expensive distractions. You want your children to have fun, but you do not want to spend all your time chasing them around. Anticipate problems. Ask yourself: "Should I let them play games before the pizza is ready? How many games should I allow them to play? How long should we stay after we finish the pizza?" Think ahead. Then tell your children exactly what you expect. Lay down the ground rules before you leave the house. Let them know what happens if they do not cooperate. Let them know what happens if they do cooperate.

> *You have had an excellent week, so we are going to Play Time Pizza for supper. You can play two video games while we are waiting for the pizza. If you listen to my directions, you can play two more games after we eat. I want you to have fun, but I also want you to behave. If you do a good job this time, I will want to take you again some day. It's up to you. We'll be leaving in ten minutes.*

You know the places where your children typically misbehave: the supermarket, church, and grandma's house. If you suspect there might be a problem, talk with your children before you leave. Tell them what you expect from them and what they can expect from you.

Think about your child's misbehavior. What are the recurring problems? What can you do to prevent these problems in the future? If your children argue, develop a plan to eliminate arguing. If your teenager is not motivated to do well in school, develop a plan that encourages motivation in school.

Proactive Shopping

Taking children shopping can be difficult. Children want everything they see. Stores are notorious for positioning items at child-eye level and within reach. Teach your children that they cannot always have everything they see. When each of our kids was about four, we would take them on practice trips to the toy store. We would explain the rules before we left:

How would you like to take a trip to the toy store?

Sure, Dad.

We are going to look and play. But we are not going to buy anything.

What do you mean?

We can go and have fun. But today is not for buying. Do you still want to go?

Yes.

We would go have fun at the toy store and leave without buying anything. They would often ask to buy something just to see if we remembered the rules. We would tell them, "Not today. Maybe some other day." We would take these practice trips about once a month. Not only were we teaching them that you can not always buy what you want, we had a lot of fun in the process.

Improving Behavior: A Step-By-Step Plan

There are many patterns in our family that I want to change but I don't know where to begin. Can you help?

The following planning guide combines many of the ideas in this book into a set of specific strategies. This is a step-by-step method of planning. Follow these steps and behavior will improve.

Step 1: Establish your goal.

How would you like things to be? What changes do you want to see in your children? When choosing a goal, base your decision on two factors.

1. Select a goal that offers a high chance of success. Your first plan must be successful. Success encourages more success. Do not start with the misbehavior that is most troublesome.
2. Select a goal that contributes to the success of the whole family. This will encourage a positive family climate.

Goal: Danny and Allison will get along with each other.

Step 2: Make a list of specific behaviors that you want to increase or decrease.

What does getting along with each other really mean? What do you expect? These are your priority behaviors:

1. Danny and Allison will argue less.
2. Danny and Allison will tease each other less.
3. Danny and Allison will share each others' toys more.
4. Danny and Allison will call each other names less.
5. Danny and Allison will cooperate more.

Step 3: Select one or two priority behaviors to change.

Choose behaviors that are easy to correct. Quick success is important.

Step 4: Observe and keep a record for five days.

Once you have selected priority behaviors, count the number of times the behaviors occur each day. Do not do anything to change the behaviors. Simply observe them. You need to know how often the behaviors are occurring before you carry out the rest of the plan. This will enable you to evaluate your success.

Assume you have selected behaviors 1 and 3. Danny and Allison will argue less. Danny and Allison will share each others' toys more. Count and record the number of times Danny and Allison argue. Count and record the number of times they share toys. Do this for five days.

By doing this you determine the current level of behavior before you begin applying consequences. This chart tells us that Danny and Allison argue an average of six times a day. They share less than once a day.

These records are very important. They will tell you if your plan is working. If you do not keep written records, you will be depending on your perception and memory. With some children, improvements come in small increments. Some improvements are not easily detected. At the start of the plan, Danny and Allison are arguing an average of six times a day. Suppose that after two weeks, they are arguing five times a day. This is a small improvement, but it is still an improvement. If left to your perceptions, you would probably say the plan is not working. You would be incorrect. You are making progress. The progress is so slight that you may not see it. Written records will show any amount of progress.

Step 5: What will you do to change the behaviors?

What reinforcements will you use? What negative consequences will you use? Make a list. Ask your children for their ideas when you explain the plan. What incentives would they like to earn? Use charts, contracts, and menus of incentives to give your plan power.

Step 6: Explain the plan to your children.

Tell them your goal. Explain the priority behaviors. Establish the rules and consequences. Clarify what you expect from them and what they can expect from you. Be positive about the plan. Tell them that this is something that is going to make everyone feel better. Tell them you are serious about the plan. You will follow through with punishments if they choose to misbehave.

> *Kids, I would like to talk to you about a new program. I expect that from now on, you will not argue. I also expect that you will share each others' toys. When you share and do not argue, you can earn extra minutes at story time. If you break a rule, you will go to time-out for five minutes. This plan will help you behave and get along with each other. I know you can do a good job.*

From that moment, the choice to behave is with Danny and Allison. Mom becomes a spectator, cheering for Danny and Allison to be winners, to be successful. When the children break a rule, Mom does not need to engage in lengthy arguments. She simply enforces the consequences. Mom is on their side. She is not the bad guy. Mom does not decide what happens. The children decide when they choose to behave or not.

Use plenty of encouragement. When your children show improvements, point out how well they are doing. Make comments that increase their self-worth. "It's good to see you sharing. You should both be proud of your behavior."

Step 7: Evaluate. Is this plan working?

Observe and keep a record as you did in Step 4. By comparing these two sets of records, you will be able to determine if your plan is effective. Get your children involved in charting. Post the chart in the kitchen. Do a new chart each week.

When your children show improvements, add another priority behavior but maintain the originals. If there is additional improvement next week, add another. Be cautious. It is better to add new behaviors slowly. Do not rush the plan or it may collapse. If there is no improvement after three weeks, adjust the plan.

Step 8: Adjust the plan.

No improvement means the expectations are too high or the consequences are not motivating. If you think the expectations are too difficult, change them. If the children are unwilling to share each other's toys, you may change your expectation to taking turns while playing a game. Begin by playing the game with them. Model sharing and taking turns. Once they are successful, let them play a game alone. This expectation still emphasizes sharing and cooperation. As they learn to play more cooperatively, try sharing toys again.

The success of any plan depends on positive feedback and incentives. Children become tired of the same reward. Change incentives as needed to maintain a high level of motivation. If your children lose interest in story time, try a new incentive, such as happy faces or stickers on a chart. Old incentives lack power.

You may be tempted to use stronger consequences if your plan shows no improvement. Stronger consequences seldom help. Stronger consequences discourage most children. Children show less effort, not more effort. It is better to be consistent with one consequence and change the positive incentives.

When behaviors do not readily change, it is not because your child is terrible. It is not because you are a failure as a parent. When a behavior fails to change, it is because the system of expectations and consequences is not working properly.

Look at the plan. Should you make changes? Are you being consistent? Have you given the plan enough time? Are you protecting your buttons? Are consequences administered quickly? Are you giving negative attention? Are you ignoring? Are you catching your children being good? These questions will help you determine where your plan can be improved.

Managing Misbehavior

Although my husband and I try to prevent misbehavior, sometimes we just blow it. What can we do to manage misbehavior?

One of the most exasperating aspects of parenthood is managing misbehavior. When we are caught up in the midst of a misbehavior event, we are not always at our emotional best, and our use of reason often disappears. Wouldn't it be nice if there were a specific, practical strategy right at your fingertips? Here is a plan that will help you determine the most effective way of managing misbehavior.

Step 1: What is the misbehavior pattern?

Most acts of misconduct occur as part of a pattern. Children develop one or more patterns of misbehavior in order to get what they want or to express an emotion. There are four typical patterns of misbehavior.

Annoying misbehaviors, such as whining, teasing, nagging, pouting, tantrums, etc.

Disobedient misbehaviors, such as not following rules, not doing chores

Defiant misbehaviors, such as refusing to listen or arguing

Aggressive misbehaviors, which can be verbal, such as name calling, put-downs; or physical, such as biting, kicking, hitting, spitting, or fighting.

Step 2: What is the purpose of the misbehavior?

Identifying the pattern points to the purpose or function of the misbehavior. Although you can never be certain of a child's motive or purpose, we know that most misbehavior does have a purpose.

When misbehavior is annoying, children may be trying to get their way. They may be trying to get you to give in or change your mind. When children are disobedient, it may be that they are not internally or externally motivated to do what you want. They may be very motivated to do something else, like ignore you. This can lead to defiance. Children who are defiant are typically after control or power. They either do not want to do what you ask or they want to do what you do not permit. Children who exhibit aggressive behavior are often expressing anger, frustration, or revenge. They may be hurt because they did not get their way or because they believe that you have done something against them.

Step 3: Take action.

Ignore annoying behaviors. This does not mean to ignore the problem. The correct action is to ignore the whining or teasing. Do not give in to demands. Tantrums need an audience. It is fine to say, "I am ignoring you." It is also helpful to use redirection. "My ears do not listen to whining, please ask in a polite voice." As a long-term solution, reinforce replacement behaviors, such as asking politely and speaking calmly.

When a child is disobedient, give a firm warning to stop. "Think about what you are doing. If you continue, there will be consequences. You decide." In other words, give a firm warning, point out that this behavior is not a good idea, and explain that he or she needs to make a better decision or punishment will occur. Explain that a poor choice will result in a negative consequence or outcome. Explain that a good choice will result in a positive consequence or outcome. "It is okay to not want to do it, but you still have to do it." Use yourself as an example. "There are times when I have to do things I do not want to do. But I still do them." As a long-term solution, reinforce replacement behaviors, such as being obedient and respectful.

Children who are defiant are usually seeking control. Remain calm. If you get upset, your child wins. Be consistent. Be prepared to follow through the first time. If you find yourself getting dragged into an argument, remember to control yourself first. Say, "I need to calm down before this goes any further. I am going to deal with me, and then I'll come back and deal with you." As a long-term solution, reinforce replacement behaviors, such as doing what is asked without an argument. "Thank you for listening the first time I asked you to take out the garbage. I appreciate it very much." "If you speak to me calmly, I will listen to what you have to say."

Minimize the effects of verbal aggression by not overreacting. This is difficult. It helps to talk with your child during a calm moment and explain the consequences of name calling—how words can hurt other's feelings. "It is okay to be upset (angry) but it is not okay to use bad words and hurt another person's feelings."

Intervene quickly to stop physical aggression. You may need to apply a time out. Once your child is calm and willing to talk, explain the consequences. Say something like, "Someone could be hurt, either physically or emotionally." Then explain that it is okay to be upset, but it is not okay to strike out. "I understand that you are angry, but it is not okay to hit." For younger children, say, "Use your words." This helps children learn to use words to express how they feel. As a long-term solution for aggression, reinforce replacement behaviors, such as playing together, sharing, speaking politely, and properly expressing anger with words or drawings. You also need to be a good example by maintaining your own emotional self-control.

Although there is no cookbook for managing misbehavior, this plan provides a simple but effective strategy. The only permanent way to improve a child's behavior is to build self-esteem. Always make this your focus. Help your children understand that we do the right thing because it feels good to do the right thing.

Teaching Kids Conflict Resolution

How can I teach my children to resolve conflicts on their own?

Children experience conflicts for many of the same reasons that adults do. Children want the circumstances in their lives to be on their own terms. They want the rules to fit their behavior rather than fit their behavior to the rules. Children can only see their own side of a situation. Children want everything to go their way. When they do not get what they want, they become angry.

It shouldn't be surprising that anytime you put two or three people who think this way into the same confined space and tell them to play and have fun, you are likely to get some conflict. So what can parents do to reduce the amount of conflict among their children? Begin by using a conflict as an opportunity to learn. Teach your children acceptable ways of expressing disappointment and resentment. Teach them how to manage their feelings without violating the other person.

> *You know, Alyssa, it's okay to be angry at your brother for teasing you. But it is not okay to hit him. What else could you have done? Let's think about other things to do when you get angry.*

This approach will not work if your child is still upset about the altercation. Communication is always more effective when everyone has had time to cool off. It also helps to intervene early before tempers erupt.

> *It sounds to me like you two may be getting into an argument. I believe that you can work this out for yourselves and I hope you do. If you need my help, let me know. But if you can't solve this on your own, you will need to take a little break from each other for a while.*

This type of message empowers your children to believe they can resolve their conflict. If you believe they can, they are likely to believe the same. Yet it also sets a limit. Knowing when to become involved and when to keep out takes judgment. As a rule, always encourage your children to solve their own conflicts. Give them time to do this. Then if you see that their conflict is escalating rather than resolving, you may need to guide them to think of a solution. Simply separate them for a few minutes, to give them time to think.

Teach your children to respect the other person even when you do not agree. This is a skill that will be helpful when they become adults. "You do not have to agree with what your brother says. He sees it his way and you see it your way. It is okay to have different opinions about this, but it's not okay to fight."

In some situations, it can also help if you add a suggestion about seeing the conflict from the other person's point of view. "Each of you has a reason for thinking that your opinion is correct." Then have the children exchange their reasons and develop a compromise. Each child has to give a little so that both can be satisfied.

As a long-term preventive, focus on the positive social behaviors in your children. Compliment your children for getting along. Parents forget this. It is easy to take good behavior for granted. This is a mistake. Look for cooperation and sharing. Then reinforce it. "I appreciate you playing together so well. Thank you. I hope you both feel proud of yourselves."

Perhaps, the most important thing a parent can do to teach their children better methods of conflict resolution is to be a good example. Model appropriate ways of solving the conflicts you encounter in your life — with your spouse, your boss, your neighbor, even the irritating sales clerk. Do not store anger; express it constructively. "When you continue to argue, I get angry because it's so frustrating to go around in circles." Show your children that there are prudent ways to disagree. Model calmness, politeness, and respect for the other person. Remember to be patient. If your children have developed patterns of arguing and fighting, it will take time to change. Hang in there. They are worth it.

Handling a Teenager

I am ready to give up on my teenager! What can I do to help my teenager behave?

The adolescent years are easier when parents and teens are willing to talk and listen to each other. Negotiation and compromise are often the key ingredients for teen and parent survival.

It is in a teenager's best interest to behave responsibly and make good decisions. That is how a teen keeps his or her parents' trust. That is also how a teen keeps his or her freedom, privileges, spending money, and car keys. For example, if your teenager wants to go to a concert but you do not want her to attend, you, as the parent, cannot stop the teen from going to the concert. She is the only one who can do that. But a teenager knows that three hours at a "forbidden" concert would not be worth it, because she would lose her parent's trust.

Teenagers need their parents' trust. They earn trust by being responsible. This sounds so simple, but we are always amazed by how few teenagers and parents understand this. For some unknown reason, teenagers seem to build a communication wall between them and their parents. Many parents and adolescents have regular, ongoing conflicts and power struggles. They argue about everything.

There is a better way. Whenever we counsel with teenagers we explain this idea:

> *This is the time in your life when you want to make your parents very happy. You want them to trust you. You want them to believe that you are a good student. You want to get good grades. You want to do a good job on your chores. You want to be polite and kind to your little brothers and sisters.*

You need to be home within your curfew. You want your parents to think you are an extremely responsible person. Because when they think you behave responsibly, then they will trust you. Then good things will happen in your life. They will allow you to do more activities because they know they can trust you. You may not believe this, but your parents really do want to do nice things for you.

We have had this talk with hundreds of adolescents over the years and almost every one has reacted with the same expression. "I never thought of it that way!" I do not think many parents think this way either. We are quick to remind these enlightened adolescents that change takes time. It will take time for them to change, but more importantly it will take time for their parents to change.

If the relationship between teens and parents has been filled with power struggles and conflicts for months or years, it will take more than a few days of responsible behavior to improve that relationship and build trust. Parents and teens need to remind each other to be patient and stay focused on positive behaviors and attitudes.

When children and teens behave properly, then it is up to parents to behave responsibly, too! Give your children encouragement and support. Look for small improvements at first. Acknowledge any step in the right direction, no matter how small. Talk with your teenagers and your younger children about the benefits of responsible behavior.

Do not forget to add that, as a bonus, when they make good decisions and behave responsibly, you feel proud of them. Teach your children that happiness comes from the inside, from doing the right thing. That is a feeling that is helpful during adolescence and the rest of your life.

Dating

My daughter wants to date before she is 16. That is against our house rules. She thinks we are being unreasonable. How can we get her to understand it is for her well being that we are doing this?

We have had these experiences already. Sometimes teenagers think that they know better than we do. Sometimes you just have to stick to your guns no matter how angry they get. They still know what the rule is and they are trying to test the boundaries. If you give in at all, even an inch, then they'll take a mile. Just reaffirm the rule and let them know that your family sticks to it. Talk to them about it. Agree to disagree if you have to. It's not easy when they're angry at you and accusing you of being unfair, but in the end you have to remember that you are the parent and they are the child.

This is a time when you can also give them other options. They can go out with a group of friends or they could come to the house and play basketball or listen to music or have pizza.

Allowing Teenage Computer Use

My teenager sometimes spends more than two hours on the computer in the evening. We don't know what he is doing, and we wish he would spend more time with us. How can we set limits on computer use?

Setting limits on computer use is identical to setting any boundary for your children. Experts suggest that a healthy process for considering appropriate boundaries begins with this question: Is this boundary or limit really for the child's benefit? Once you have set your own feelings and prejudices aside and considered the developmental stage of your child, you are better equipped to set any limits or boundaries.

To help your children learn to use the computer safely and wisely, first consider what is appropriate for his/her stage of development.

Infants/toddlers: This stage is easy because young children do not have the skills to surf the Internet or load computer games. Computer use at this stage will be limited to what you and your child can do together and simple games or stories your child can control on his or her own.

Children: Cyberspace and computer games are mostly inappropriate for children. Wise parents protect their children from excessive advertising, sex, and violence by providing secure filtering software and wholesome computer games. We also suggest setting up the computer in a central location so you can monitor and protect your child from inappropriate material.

Teens: If you have a teenager, you probably already know about instant messaging, chat rooms, and other popular pastimes the Internet has to offer. So where do you draw the line for your teen? The first step is to find out about what your teen wants to explore via the computer and then consider what is appropriate given his/her stage of development. We tend to err on the side of protecting our teens from words and pictures that they do not have the judgment or wisdom to understand. In our experience, instant messaging can become a forum for harmful gossiping, so we have not allowed our children to participate.

We also suggest that you move the computer out of his bedroom and into a central location so you can monitor where is he going on the web. Have him tell you how much time he needs to spend on the computer doing school work, then agree on an appropriate amount of time for recreation.

When a family needs to share a computer, we've found that a posted schedule works well. This is something you could cover at your weekly family meeting. Start by scheduling any time each family member needs for schoolwork or other business. Then have each family member select the extra blocks of time. Make sure that you set a policy for when someone can get on the computer when it is free, and what the daily time limit is.

Sharing Household Chores

My husband doesn't lift a finger with the kids or around the house. After a long day I find myself resentful that he won't pitch in more. What can I do?

It's all in the way you ask your husband. When you do it under stress and you're angry and demanding and upset and you get to that boiling point, no one is going to do what you want them to do...especially your husband. It's all about validation. When you validate him, he can validate you. Many of us women think that our husbands are supposed to know exactly what we are thinking, but they don't. They think differently than we do. A lot of times when I am angry about something I have found that it is my fault because I have not told Brent what I need. When you voice it to them in a kind manner, like "Hey could you take out the trash while I change the baby's diaper?," that helps. Sometimes, as women, we ask men to do a job, say the dishes, but they may not do everything the way we would. We're already angry and resentful so we criticize their job – maybe the way they loaded the dishwasher or that they failed to wipe down the counters – and that makes them not want to help because they feel like they can't do it right. I've learned that I need to be appreciative of whatever Brent does and validate him for it and, in return, I get more help.

CHAPTER 13

"WE'RE BETTER OFF APART": WHEN DIVORCE IS THE ONLY ANSWER

Parenting does not stop when couples with children divorce. Rather there are new challenges and opportunities. With almost 50 percent of marriages in America ending in divorce, we know that this is an area that needs to be addressed in our book. However, since we have been married for over 20 years, we admit that we aren't authorities on the subject. So we decided to consult with an expert. Dr. Sal Severe has decades of experience counseling parents, children, and teens affected by divorce and has generously contributed his wisdom to this section of *Raising a G-Rated Family in an X-Rated World*. Whether you are divorced or not, Dr. Severe's stories, suggestions, and insights can help us all become better and more empathetic parents.

My husband and I are getting divorced. What thoughts and feelings do children usually have about divorce, and how do their feelings affect their behavior?

Here are some stories and ideas that may help you learn more about the way children think and feel about their parents' divorce:

> Lisa was the kind of student teachers would call on when they wanted an imaginative answer. She had a reputation for being a child with a cheery and sociable disposition.

> She was blessed with intelligence, personality, and self-confidence. She earned good grades and was a leader among her peers. The world was an exciting place for Lisa. She was optimistic and enthusiastic about her life and her future.
>
> Then her life changed — suddenly and almost completely. She went from honor student to school failure, from cheerful to depressed, from leader to social recluse. She became unsure of herself, inattentive, forgetful, and depressed. School was simply not that important to her any more.
>
> What caused this dreadful transformation? Lisa was suffering from an affliction that has no name but strikes as many as 80 percent of the children in some schools. Lisa's parents got a divorce.

When asked about how she felt about her parent's divorce, she insisted that she didn't care and wasn't having any problems with it. Lisa's reaction is typical. Like most children who experience the distress of divorce, she could not explain why she was doing poorly in school and she did not want anyone to know she was hurting inside. She did not want to say anything that may aggravate the difficulties at home any further. Children see the stress their parents are going through. They fear that exposing their emotions will only add to everyone's misery. This is the reason that most children never talk to their parents about their feelings concerning the divorce. These hidden feelings increase anxiety and weaken a child's ability to perform in school. Additionally, repressed feelings may become the seeds for larger problems later in life.

We asked Lisa:

> *What do you think about your parents getting divorced?*
>
> *I don't like it.*
>
> *What do you mean?*

My mom cries a lot.

How does that make you feel?

Sad. I wish she would stop.

Do you know why your parents got divorced?

They used to fight a lot.

Did they ever fight about you?

Yes.

Do you feel it was your fault that your parents got divorced?

Yes. It was all my fault.

With these words, tears filled Lisa's remorse-filled eyes. She wept openly for several minutes. She was dumping some of the emotional garbage she had been carrying for months. When she caught her breath, she explained:

> *One time I was standing in front of the TV and my dad yelled at me to move. Then my mom yelled at him to stop yelling at me. Then they got in a big fight and my dad left the house. Two weeks later they told me they were getting a divorce. So I think they are getting a divorce because of me.*

Lisa was overcome by guilt. She was feeling responsible for her parents' divorce. Over half of the children we speak with feel that they were the primary reason for the divorce. They think, "If only I had been better behaved or done a better job on my chores. If only I had kept my room clean or gotten better grades, my parents would still be together. If I would have been a better child, none of this would have happened." Children blame themselves. This can create overwhelming feelings of poor self-worth, insecurity, and depression. When a child feels guilty or depressed, school is simply not that important.

Twenty-five years ago, the divorce rate was not high enough to merit much attention. It's different today and we have learned a lot along the way. Divorce hurts children and hurt children strike back, sometimes at themselves. Loss, rejection, abandonment, loneliness, fear, guilt, stress, and anger hit hard. Most observers see a connection between the divorce rate and increased rates of gang delinquency, drug use, and dropouts.

Children psychologically bond with both parents. When parents divorce, children may feel like their personality has been torn in half. Children feel like half of their "self" is missing. These feelings of loss, rejection, and abandonment destroy a child's ability to concentrate in school.

These unhealthy feelings increase when parents attack or degrade each other. When one parent says malicious things about the other parent in front of the children, the children worry that these displeasing qualities exist in themselves. "If Dad is a bad person, am I a bad person too? After all, I'm a lot like my dad."

When parents try to get even or outdo each other, the children become confused. We worked with one family in which the mother insisted that the children be sheltered from violence. A reasonable request. Dad's favorite weekend activities were "body-count" movies and afternoon trips to the rifle range. While the parents argued about what was best for the children, the children became divided and emotionally unsteady.

Some children of divorce lose contact with one of their parents. Nathan's parents have been divorced for five years. His father has remarried and has children with his new wife. Over the years, Nathan has gradually lost his relationship with his father.

I feel like no one likes me.

Do you feel that way because your dad doesn't see you?

Yes.

What do you mean?

It must be me. He doesn't like me for some reason.

Do you think you have done something wrong?

I must have done something. Maybe I'm a bad kid.

Do you think you are a bad kid?

Yes.

How often do you feel that way?

All the time.

How often do you think about your father?

Every day.

Nathan's feelings of rejection and loss cut deep. He believed that he was a worthless child. He was sure that his lack of paternal contact meant that he was not worthy of his father's love and time. He thought about it every day. His lack of self worth interfered with every aspect of his life. He was afraid to make friends. He was afraid to do well in school. He was even afraid to get too close to his mother. If his father did not care, if his father left him, others would too.

Some children worry about being abandoned by the caretaking parent. "My dad has left me, how do I know my mom won't leave me?" "Who will take care of me?" This is another reason children do not talk to their parents about their feelings. A seven-year-old once explained, "My mom is very angry at my dad. If I tell her how sad I am, she will get madder. Then she might leave me, too." Children are afraid to say or do anything that will alienate or provoke their parents for fear that both may leave.

Anger and aggression are typical reactions to divorce. This is especially true when the parents get angry at each other. Steven's parents had been divorced for several months. During that time, Steven had been getting more aggressive at school and at home. What caused the increased anger and aggression? Steven was angry at his dad. Angry for leaving.

Angry for not spending more time with him. Angry for having a new girlfriend. Steven did not direct his anger at his dad. That might drive his dad away even more. Steven took it out on peers, because it was relatively safe to do so. He also took his anger out on his little sister, because she liked their dad's new girlfriend.

Steven was also angry at his father because there wasn't as much money as there once was. "I'm mad because we are poor now. We can't do things like we used to. My dad has all the money." Children soon learn that divorce lowers financial status. Children worry about basic needs and routine. "How will we buy food? Will we have to move into a cheaper home? When will I ever get some new clothes? What about the new bike I was supposed to get? Can I still be on the basketball team?" Children worry about money and the changes that lower income will bring.

Change frightens children. Often, one parent takes the children and leaves home. They may move in with relatives or into less expensive quarters. For many children, this means a new home, new school, new friends, and new stresses. Add this to the loss of a parent and radical change in lifestyle and you have the ingredients for an emotional trauma. These changes interfere with success in school and almost every aspect of a child's life.

Some children fear being stolen by an angry or vengeful parent. This fear develops when parents make threats or hostile remarks. "I'll take the kids away from you and you'll never see them again." The thought of never seeing their mother or father again is frightening. This often occurs when one parent is denied access to the children. As a result, children are afraid to walk to school, walk home, or be in a situation where they might be kidnapped.

Children hope their parents will get back together. It is understandable for children to think in this manner. Children want the family to be the way it used to be. This is a fantasy that most children grasp onto regardless of the facts. A college freshman once told us that he frequently thinks about reuniting his parents. They have been divorced since he was six and both parents have been remarried for years. He still hangs on to the possibility.

Delayed Effects

The aftermath of divorce lasts for years. Melody had always done well in school. She was a well-behaved and trustworthy young lady. Within a two-month period, it all turned around. Melody quit going to school, became promiscuous, and got involved with drugs. Yet Melody knew exactly what was going on inside. She was angry at her father. He left her and her mother when Melody was seven. Melody kept hoping he would return. If he did, she wanted to be sure he would be proud of her, so she always did well for him. Then recently, she realized he was never coming back. "So why be good? I decided to stop working so hard and have a good time instead."

It had been ten years since Melody's father left. It took ten years for the hurt and loss to fester to the point where it finally erupted. It took ten years for the effects to become visible. It would be easy to dismiss a ten-year-old event as probable cause for a recent change in behavior. We now realize that the impact of divorce may be immediate or may not surface for years. Parents and teachers must be aware of this when working with troubled children. Do not overlook a divorce as influencing a child's behavior or mood just because it happened several years ago. It may still be fresh in the child's mind.

Monday Morning Re-Entry

The most common debilitating effect of divorce is Monday morning re-entry after a weekend with dad or mom. Many children of divorce see their non-custodial parent only on weekends, usually two weekends a month. Upon returning from the weekend visit, many children go through a period of adjustment that may last for several days. Some children withdraw, daydream, and show a lack of motivation. Other children act out or become short tempered, belligerent, and oppositional. Some children become vengeful and aggressive.

Several years ago, when divorce was less common, teachers and parents assumed that the Monday-morning re-entry behavior was caused by a weekend of freedom with no limits and no discipline. The popular conclusion was that the children should see less of the non-custodial parent. It is true that weekend parents have a tendency to indulge their children; however, Monday morning re-entry is the result of something else.

We now realize that Monday morning re-entry is likely caused by seeing too little of the weekend parent. There are at least two reasons for this. First, a weekend is barely enough time to get acquainted with someone on an intimate or affectionate level. Just as the parent and children start warming up to each other, it's over. The children relive the loss of a parent every other Sunday night. Since it takes several days to deal with this loss, the re-entry behaviors result.

Second, many weekend parents feel like outsiders in their children's lives. The parent and children do not see enough of each other to learn each other's likes, dislikes, interests, emotions, or patterns of behavior. Weekend parents do not get to know their children, and weekend children do not get to know their parent. The result: the Disneyland syndrome. Weekend parents have a tendency to pack the weekend with expensive, fun-filled activities, gifts, and junk food. This does two things. It tells the children that this parent is nice. It also eliminates any need for routine discipline. Children do not misbehave when they are being stuffed with goodies and entertainment.

What's the cure? More time with the weekend parent. Increased contact eliminates the feelings of loss and the re-entry behaviors are diminished. More time with the weekend parent also neutralizes the Disneyland effects. As this parent becomes more involved with the children, more routine activities will occur. This parent will develop a wider view of the children's lives and will become more committed to all aspects of the children, including discipline. This usually leads to more cooperation and consistency between the parents. The result is a more stable environment for the children. The children end up doing better for both parents and better in school as well.

What Parents Can Do: A Child's Three Wishes

The effects of divorce on children cannot be eliminated, but their impact can be reduced. What follows is a list of optimal circumstances which may not always be easy for parents to accomplish, but are always best for children.

Wish 1. Children should have free access to both parents.

They should be able to phone or see either parent without fear of offending the other parent. Children should not have to choose between parents. This creates a lose-lose situation. Choose one and lose the other. Children need permission to love each parent in front of the other parent.

What about the circumstances in which one parent is far away? Many absent parents mistakenly believe that the children they left behind are better off without them. Not true. Encourage as much contact as possible. Write letters and make phone calls. Make cassettes or video tapes. Children love e-mail. Send pictures. Ask for copies of school reports and invitations to events. Visit on holidays and summer vacations. The more contact the better.

If a parent refuses contact with a child, explain to the child that it is not his or her fault. Lack of contact does not make the child a worthless person. Provide frequent reassurance by pointing out the lovable qualities in the child.

There are some situations where contact should be restricted. For example, a parent who has abused the children should have supervised visitations.

Wish 2. Children want consistency in order to feel safe and secure.

Parents need to establish similar rules and consequences at both homes. Parents need to periodically discuss and agree on daily routine, such as allowable foods and snacks, movies, bed time, bath time, homework, church, etc. A cooperative spirit tells children that both parents are likable people. Children want nice parents as much as parents want nice children. Consistency gives children balance and helps them adjust to the divorce situation.

Many single parents feel guilty. Guilty parents have a tendency to give-in to misbehaviors. They make excuses. "It's not his fault. He is confused right now." Giving in to misbehavior is a mistake. Be consistent. Be understanding and supportive, but do not let children misbehave. Children need limits and consistency.

Wish 3. Children should know that both parents are still involved in their lives.

Parents do not divorce their children. Children need dual parenting. This goes beyond joint custody. Children need both parents actively participating in all aspects of their lives, especially school. Both parents should attend teacher conferences, if not together then separately. Both parents should attend school functions. They can sit apart or take turns going to events. Dual involvement clearly indicates that both parents believe that school is a priority. This makes doing well in school more important to the child.

What Schools Can Do

Schools have a responsibility to stay in touch with both parents, even if the custodial parent does not like it. Schools should provide a model for best practice. Since children do better when both parents are involved in the education process, schools need to make every effort to include both parents. Ask the school to send two report cards. Set up two parent conferences. Send two invitations to school events. Call both parents when the child has a good day. This will create a more stable and supportive home-school-home environment.

Teachers should also be aware that children of divorce often exhibit emotional and behavioral problems. Teachers should provide support and encouragement during difficult times. They should be good listeners and allow time for the child to talk about feelings. A teacher may be the only adult with whom he is willing to talk.

Millions of American children have been hurt by divorce. Until recently, we assumed that the natural flexibility and resiliency built into all children would guarantee their survival. We now know differently. Children must feel good about themselves in order to behave and to perform well in school. Emotional conflict, anxiety, stress, and fear interrupt the natural growth process.

Children adjust to divorce better and therefore do better in school when both parents are part of their lives. There is no cure for divorce, but there is treatment. Keep peace between the parents and keep both parents in the children's lives. The greater the harmony between parents, the better the adjustment for the children. It's that simple. Many parents who have been through a hostile divorce may think that these suggestions are unrealistic. That may be so. We are suggesting what is best for children. What is best for children is peace, harmony, and communication between parents.

Chapter 14

"Take Ten": Our Top Ten Parenting Lists

No one can be a great parent all the time. That's why we sometimes have to "take ten." Besides taking a few minutes alone, we've found that these "top ten" lists help us put things in perspective. We hope they work for you, too.

Top Ten Parenting Principles

1. *Pay off correct behavior, not misbehavior.* Reinforce polite requests, not whining, teasing, and tantrums. Reinforce calm discussions, not arguments and power struggles.
2. *Think before you talk.* Say what you mean. Mean what you say. Follow through. Give yourself visual reminders. Reward yourself for being consistent.
3. *Expect good behavior from your children.* Children must know what you expect from them and what they can expect from you. When children can predict how you will behave in given situations, they make better choices.
4. *Children believe what you tell them.* Coach your children on ways to be successful. Teach your children that effort is essential to success. Use plenty of encouragement. When you encourage your children, they will see that you have faith and confidence in them. Encouragement will help your children face situations with more confidence.

5. *Anticipate problems.* Tell your children the rules in advance. Be specific. Be reasonable. Once you recognize a misbehavior pattern, establish a plan. Spotlight success. Provide support and encouragement. Use charts and contracts to strengthen your plan.
6. *Use punishments that teach decision-making and accountability.* Children survive reasonable punishments, such as restriction and time out. Do not punish when you are angry. Do not punish to get even. Relate punishment to your child's decisions about misbehavior. This teaches responsibility.
7. *Begin teaching responsibility and decision-making when your children are young.* Prepare your children to live in the real world. Be strict but positive. Children need limits and structure. Children need ground rules. They need consistency. Children see these qualities as an expression of your love and concern.
8. *Love your children regardless of their behavior.* Focus on your children's positive qualities. Teach your children to seek self reward — to feel good about doing the right thing. Look for praiseworthy decisions. Teach your children to like themselves. Teach them to understand their weaknesses and accept their faults. Use yourself as an example. They will learn to admit their shortcomings to others. As a result, their weaknesses will have less power in their lives.
9. *Support yourself, even when others sit in judgment.* Do not let your children push your buttons. Be strong. Control your own behavior to be a good model. Your children learn from you.
10. *Provide a healthy and pleasant family climate.* Emphasize each other's strengths. Accept each other's weaknesses. Talk about values and goals. Your children will learn to come to you with their problems. This will come in handy when they are teenagers.

Top Ten Characteristics of Successful Parents

Successful parents:

1. *Welcome change in themselves and their children.* They see change as positive. They seek self-improvement. But they also have patience, for they recognize that it takes time to see change in themselves and their children.
2. *Possess good judgment.* They know the difference between mischief and misconduct.
3. *Have a sense of humor about raising children.*
4. *Believe that discipline is a teaching process.* It's not simply punishment. Discipline is everything we do to teach children to be responsible and think for themselves.
5. *Focus on the positive attitudes and behavior in their children.* They call attention to positive qualities.
6. *Use self-esteem as motivation.* "You made a good choice. You should be proud of yourself!"
7. *Behave themselves.* They provide good example by being responsible, not perfect.
8. *Behave consistently.* They say what they mean and mean what they say. They follow through. They do not give in to misbehavior demands.
9. *Behave proactively.* They anticipate problems and plan to avoid them.
10. *Stay calm when their button is being pushed.* They understand that anger gets in the way and makes conflicts worse.

Top Ten Parenting Misbehaviors

1. *Thinking only one-way.*
2. *Responding inconsistently.*
3. *Not seeing the difference between misconduct and mischief.*
4. *Reacting emotionally.*
5. *Providing a poor example.*
6. *Taking good behavior and good attitude for granted.*
7. *Equating discipline and punishment.*
8. *Lacking patience.*
9. *Forgetting to have fun with their children.*
10. *Not cherishing the wonders of parenting.*

Top Ten Ways to Be More Consistent

1. *Increase your awareness.* Consistency is important every minute.
2. *Remember the strong relationship between consistency and behavior.*
3. *Understand that consistency is a true expression of love and caring.*
4. *Have patience.*
5. *Specify target behaviors.*
6. *Give yourself visible, tangible reminders.*
7. *Support each other.*
8. *Plan to be tested — don't make excuses.*
9. *Choose to have a good time.*
10. *Reward yourself.*

Appendix 1

Resources: Where To Find G-Rated Media

These web sites can help you find movies, videos, DVDs, CDs, or video games, and books appropriate for your family.

Movies

United States Conference of Catholic Bishops

Parents of all backgrounds can benefit from the United States Conference of Catholic Bishops' (USCCB) web site. It provides thoughtful movie reviews that answer the following questions for movie goers:

- How much sex and violence does this film show?
- What sorts of values and morals do the themes of this movie promote?
- How does this movie relate to current Catholic beliefs?
- Is the film appropriate for children?
- What would sensitive adults think of this movie?

The USCCB has its own movie ratings that are clearly explained at the end of each review.

http://www.usccb.org/movies/ or www.usccb.org

Grading the Movies

"Grading the Movies" was launched over ten years ago. Back then, it was a weekly newspaper column with an easy letter grading system and a 350-word review of any newly released video. Now the same easy-to-read format is on the Internet, and it continues to provide "…families with the tools they need to make informed media decisions." Please note that while the Grading the Movies writers (all parents) constantly produce new movie and video reviews, they have stopped reviewing music and video games. However, you can still access their extensive archive of music and video game reviews.

www.gradingthemovies.com

Focus on the Family

The Focus on the Family organization maintains a comprehensive web site offering parents information on the spiritual content, sexual content, violent content, crude or profane language, and drug and alcohol content of movies, videos, DVDs, and television shows.

www.pluggedinonline.com

Parents Television Council

The Parents Television Council (PTC) has nearly one million members, and they are dedicated to "…bringing America's demand for positive, family-oriented television programming to the entertainment industry." The PTC web site will help you choose appropriate television shows for your family and provide you with general information about children and the media. If you want to campaign to make media more G-Rated, this is an organization to join.

www.parentstv.org

The Dove Foundation

The non-profit Dove Foundation awards a Dove Seal to any movie or video rated "family-friendly" by its film review board. These folks are strict and we love 'em for it! While all family-oriented reviewers will tell you whether the "f word" is said, the Dove review board reports exactly how many times the word is uttered. At the Dove Foundation web site you can read reviews and purchase "family approved" films and "family edited" versions of films.

www.dove.org

Screen It!

Some of you will be annoyed by all the "pop-up ads" on the Screen It! entertainment review web site; however, the extremely easy-to-read movie/video review chart will delight and inform all of you. The Screen It! reviewers analyze 15 different aspects of each film or video. Find out about everything from "tense family scenes" to violence, sex, and smoking. A glance at the Screen It! chart will tell you whether a movie contains mild, moderate, extreme, or none of the particular category. The site also provides music reviews. For those of us highly annoyed by ads, there's an ad-free subscription version of Screen It!

www.screenit.com

Video Games

Edutaining Kids

Hand-held computer games are rated from E to A (for Everyone to Adults only), but your idea of what is for "everyone" may not be the same as the rating board's idea, and that is why edutaining.com is so helpful. The site recommends appropriate games and discusses content.

www.edutainingkids.com

Books, Music, and Games

Review Corner

This web site provides lists of "best" children's books, music, DVDs, toys, games, and more. The reviewers put all media through a number of tests by children and adults to establish their ratings.

www.reviewcorner.com

If you need wholesome books and music in a hurry, look for products that have won awards or have been included on lists of "good" books created by trusted organizations. On the next few pages are suggestions for how to find award-winning books and music.

Look for Award Winners

The American Library Association (ALA) bestows awards each year for the best books for children and young adults in various divisions ranging from picture books to young adult non-fiction titles. The Newbery Medal (for the best story) and Caldecott Medal (for the best illustrations) are the most well known because the books that have won either of these prizes usually carry a replica of the medal on their covers. If you are looking for wholesome, enduring titles for your children and teens, begin by getting a list of Newbery and/or Caldecott Medal winners. (The award-winning books are easy to find in most libraries.) Some of the Newbery Medal winners, which are often for older children and young adults, may address mature topics that are thought provoking, so you should preview each title yourself to make sure your child is ready for the subject. However, these well-written, thoughtfully developed books are a great way to open a discussion about particular topics with your children. The ALA web site (www.ala.org) maintains a list of past and current winners.

Consult a Trustworthy List

The following books offer up-to-date lists of wholesome reading material for children and teens:

Books to Build On, John Holdren and E.D. Hirsch Jr., Delta Trade Books, 1996.

The New Read-Aloud Handbook, Jim Trelease, Penguin, 1995.

The New York Times Parent's Guide to the Best Books for Children, Eden Ross Lipson, Times Books, 1991 (updated and revised often).

Straight Talk About Reading, Susan L. Hall and Louisa C. Moats, Contemporary Books, 1999.

Booksellers such as Amazon and Barnes and Noble offer lists of popular children's books, so try those web sites or use an Internet search engine to search for "best children's books."

For wholesome children's music, http://www.bestchildrensmusic.com/, offers selections for all ages. This web site is endorsed by major national parenting and educational organizations.

Appendix 2

Footnotes and References

[1] Victoria J. Rideout, Elizabeth A. Vendewater, and Ellen A. Wartella. "Zero to Six: Electronic Media in the Lives of Infants, Toddlers, and Preschoolers." Menlo Park, CA: The Henry J. Kaiser Family Foundation, Fall 2003.

[2] Ibid.

[3] Wolf, Naomi. *The Beauty Myth*. New York: William Morrow and Company, Inc., 1991.

[4] "*Sports Illustrated:* A 50-Year Perspective." CNN/*Sports Illustrated,* 2003.

[5] "*Sports Illustrated's* 'Fresh Face.'" CNN/*Sports Illustrated,* 2003.

[6] Kunkel, Dale. "Sex On TV: Content and Context." Menlo Park, CA: Kaiser Family Foundation, 2001.

[7] Ibid.

[8] News Release. Menlo Park, CA: Kaiser Family Foundation, February 6, 2001.

[9] "Kids & Media." Menlo Park, CA: Kaiser Family Foundation, November 1999.

[10] "Children & Television: Frequently Asked Questions." Washington, D.C.: Center for Media Education, 2003.

[11] American Center for Law & Justice. Issue Spotlight: Pornography.

[12] "TV Violence." Washington, D.C.: Center of Media Education, 2003.

[13] "Fair Play? Violence, Gender, and Race in Video Games." Oakland, CA: Children NOW, December 2001.

[14] "Violence on Television—What Do Children Learn? What Can Parents Do?" Washington, D.C.: American Psychological Association, 2003.

[15] Glaubke, Christina R., et al. "Fair Play?: Violence, Gender and Race in Video Games." Oakland, CA: Children NOW, 2001.

[16] Bok, Sissela. *Mayhem*. Reading, MA: Perseus Books Group, 1998.

[17] Center for Media Education. "Children & Television: Frequently Asked Questions." Washington, D.C., 1997.

[18] Bok, Sissela. *Mayhem*. Reading, MA: Perseus Books Group, 1998.

[19] "Statement of Chairman Robert Pitofsky on FTC Youth Violence Report, September 13, 2000." Senate Commerce Committee.

[20] Montgomery, Kathryn, C. "Digital Kids: The New On-Line Children's Consumer Culture." Washington, D.C.: Center for Media Education, 2003.

[21] Center for Media Education. "Children & Television: Frequently Asked Questions." Washington, D.C., 1997.

[22] Ibid.

[23] Ibid.

[24] Montgomery, Kathryn C. "Digital Kids: The New On-Line Children's Consumer Culture." Washington, D.C.: Center for Media Education, 2003.

[25] Faber, Adele and Elaine Mazlish. *How to Talk So Kids Will Listen & Listen So Kids Will Talk*. New York: HarperCollins, 2002.

[26] Severe, Sal. *How to Behave So Your Children Will, Too!* Tempe, AZ: Greentree Publishing, 1997.

[27] Ibid.

[28] Ibid.

[29] Ibid.

[30] Ibid.

[31] Riley, Sue Spayth. *How to Generate Values in Young Children*. Washington, D.C.: National Association for the Education of Young Children, 1984.

Index